MY BEST YEAR YET

365 DAY, 5 MINUTE DAILY FAITH DEVOTIONAL FOR TEEN BOYS

Who Want to Build Confidence, Courage, and Character—One Daily Truth at a Time.

JANUARY 1

WHO GOD SAYS I AM

Yet to all who did receive him, to those who believed in his name, he gave the right to become children of God— **John 1:12**

DEVOTIONAL

You are cherished and valued by God, and your identity is rooted in His love, not in the opinions of others.

Who do you believe you are when you look in the mirror? What does God say about your identity that can change how you see yourself?

PRAYER

God, help me to understand who I am in You. Open my heart to embrace the truth of my identity as Your beloved creation. Please guide me to live confidently in Your love.

I am not defined by my mistakes, but by the love that God has for me.

JANUARY 2

MADE FOR A PURPOSE

For we are God's handiwork, created in Christ Jesus to do good works, which God prepared in advance for us to do. **Ephesians 2:10**

DEVOTIONAL

Each of us has our own unique journey, and recognizing our individual purpose helps us bloom into who we are meant to become.

What do you believe your unique talents and passions say about the purpose you were made for? How can you start exploring them more deeply this week?

PRAYER

God, thank You for creating me with intention and for a purpose. Help me discover my gifts and show me how to use them to make a difference in the world around me. Amen.

You are not an accident; you are a masterpiece in the making.

JANUARY 3

STRENGTH IN WEAKNESS

But he said to me, "My grace is sufficient for you, for my power is made perfect in weakness." Therefore I will boast all the more gladly about my weaknesses, so that Christ's power may rest on me. **2 Corinthians 12:9**

DEVOTIONAL

True strength often emerges from the very weaknesses we wish to hide; embracing them can lead to remarkable growth and connection.

What are some weaknesses or struggles in your life that you often try to hide or overcome on your own? How might embracing those moments of vulnerability help you grow stronger?

PRAYER

God, thank You for being my strength when I feel weak. Help me to remember that in my moments of struggle, You are right there with me, lifting me up. Give me courage to embrace my weaknesses and trust in Your strength.

Our weaknesses can be the starting point of our greatest victories.

JANUARY 4

LOVED NO MATTER WHAT

The Lord is good, a refuge in times of trouble.
He cares for those who trust in him. **Nahum 1:7**

DEVOTIONAL

Even when we feel cast aside or unworthy, there is a profound love that embraces us for who we are, reminding us of our worth.

What are some moments in your life when you've felt loved the most, and how can you remember that love even when times get tough?

PRAYER

God, thank you for your unwavering love that surrounds me every day. Help me to feel that love deep in my heart and share it with others no matter the challenges I face. Amen.

You are loved beyond your greatest flaw and celebrated for who you are

JANUARY 5

MY FAITH IS MY OWN

"So then, each of us will give an account of ourselves to God."
Romans 14:12

DEVOTIONAL
Your faith journey is distinct and personal; nurture it just as you would a dear friendship.

What does it mean for you to have a faith that is uniquely yours, beyond what your family or friends believe? In what moments have you felt your faith truly shine?

PRAYER
Dear God, thank you for guiding me on this journey of faith. Help me to embrace what I believe and to share it boldly with others. Amen.

Faith isn't something you're born into; it's something you grow into.

JANUARY 6

JESUS: MY ROLE MODEL

"In your relationships with one another, have the same mindset as Christ Jesus." **Philippians 2:5**

DEVOTIONAL
True role models, like Jesus, inspire us not just through their achievements but through their love and service to others.

What qualities do you admire most about Jesus, and how can you apply those qualities in your life each day?

PRAYER
Dear Jesus, help me to look to You as my ultimate role model. Guide me in emulating Your kindness, strength, and love in my everyday actions. Thank You for being the perfect example to follow.

Be the kind of man who leads with love and strength, just like Jesus taught us.

I'M A WORK IN PROGRESS

Being confident of this, that he who began a good work in you will carry it on to completion until the day of Christ Jesus. **Philippians 1:6**

DEVOTIONAL
Remember, just like a beautiful quilt that is made over time, our lives, too, are stitched with experiences and lessons, each contributing to our unique tapestry.

What are some areas in your life where you feel like you're still growing? How can you embrace that journey instead of getting frustrated with where you are?

PRAYER
Dear God, thank You for making me who I am today and for the potential You're continuing to grow in me. Help me to trust the process and to see the beauty in my journey of becoming.

Every masterpiece was once a work in progress.

CREATED ON PURPOSE

For I know the plans I have for you," declares the Lord, "plans to prosper you and not to harm you, plans to give you hope and a future. **Jeremiah 29:11**

DEVOTIONAL
Just like Sam, remember that every challenge you face is shaping you for the purpose you were uniquely designed for.

What unique talents or interests do you have that make you feel excited to be you? How can you use those gifts to make a difference in your life and the lives of others?

PRAYER
God, thank you for creating me with purpose. Help me to see and embrace the plans you have for my life and to walk boldly in the path you've set before me. Amen.

You were designed with intention, and your life has a unique mission.

BELONGING TO GOD

See what great love the Father has lavished on us, that we should be called children of God! And that is what we are! The reason the world does not know us is that it did not know him. **1 John 3:1**

DEVOTIONAL
In God's eyes, you are always loved and belonging,
no matter where life takes you.

What does it mean to you personally to belong to God? How does knowing you're part of something greater affect your daily choices and your relationships with others?

PRAYER
Dear God, thank you for embracing me as your own and for always being there for me. Help me to understand what it truly means to belong to You and to live my life reflecting that love. Amen.

Belonging to God is like having an unbreakable bond that connects your heart to His.

JANUARY 10

STANDING OUT, NOT BLENDING IN

As iron sharpens iron, so one person sharpens another.
Proverbs 27:17

DEVOTIONAL
Dare to be true to yourself, for your unique colors can
inspire and uplift those around you.

What does it mean to you to stand out in a world that often encourages you to blend in? Are there specific areas in your life where you feel called to be different, even if it might feel uncomfortable?

PRAYER
Dear God, help me embrace the uniqueness you've given me. Guide me to have the courage to stand out for what's right, and let my light shine brightly in the world around me.

Being yourself is the bravest thing you can do.

JANUARY 11

DOING WHAT'S RIGHT WHEN NO ONE SEES

The integrity of the upright guides them, but the unfaithful are destroyed by their duplicity. **Proverbs 11:3**

DEVOTIONAL
Integrity shines brightly in a world where choices can be made without accountability; true character is revealed not in moments of praise, but in the quiet decisions made when no one is watching.

What does it mean for you to do the right thing when no one is watching, and how can you keep yourself accountable in those moments? Think about a recent situation where you made a choice, and ask yourself if you would have acted differently if someone else had been present.

PRAYER
Dear God, help me to choose what's right even when I think no one is watching. Fill my heart with courage and integrity so that I may honor you in every choice I make. Amen.

Integrity is doing the right thing, even when no one is watching.

JANUARY 12

BEING HONEST IN ALL THINGS

The Lord detests lying lips, but he delights in people who are trustworthy.
Proverbs 12:22

DEVOTIONAL
By embracing honesty, we nurture our integrity, fostering genuine relationships and self-respect that will serve us well through all stages of life.

What does it mean to you to be honest, even when it's tough? Can you think of a time when being truthful was hard but ultimately led to a better outcome? How did it feel to own your truth?

PRAYER
God, help us to embrace honesty in all areas of our lives. May we find the courage to speak our truth and the wisdom to listen. Amen.

Integrity is doing the right thing, even when no one is watching.

JANUARY 13

MY WORD MATTERS

My dear brothers and sisters, take note of this: Everyone should be quick to listen, slow to speak and slow to become angry, because human anger does not produce the righteousness that God desires. **James 1:19-20**

DEVOTIONAL

Words have the power to either lift someone up or bring them down, so always choose to speak positively and kindly.

What words do you speak or keep silent that truly reflect who you are and what you believe? How can you ensure that your words are building others up rather than tearing them down?

PRAYER

God, thank You for the gift of my voice. Help me to choose my words wisely and to use them to encourage others and reflect Your love.

Your words have the power to shape the world around you.

JANUARY 14

COURAGE IN EVERYDAY LIFE

Have I not commanded you? Be strong and courageous. Do not be afraid; do not be discouraged, for the Lord your God will be with you wherever you go. **Joshua 1:9**

DEVOTIONAL

Courage isn't about never feeling afraid; it's about pressing on in spite of your fears and finding strength in the support of those around you.

What does courage look like for you in your daily life? Think about a moment when you felt scared or unsure. How did you find the strength to face that challenge?

PRAYER

Dear God, help me to find courage in the small moments of my life. Give me the strength to take brave steps, even when I feel afraid. Thank you for always being with me.

Courage isn't the absence of fear, but the decision to move forward despite it.

RESISTING PEER PRESSURE

Am I now trying to win the approval of human beings, or of God? Or am I trying to please people? If I were still trying to please people, I would not be a servant of Christ. **Galatians 1:10**

DEVOTIONAL

Staying true to your beliefs and values, even when it feels lonely, is a testament to your character and can inspire others to do the same.

What situations have you faced recently where you felt pressure to conform? How did you respond, and what could you do differently next time?

PRAYER

Dear God, help me stand strong against the pressure to fit in. Give me wisdom and courage to make choices that reflect who You've made me to be. Amen.

True strength is choosing to be authentic, even when it feels hard.

JANUARY 16

PRACTICING SELF-CONTROL

For the Spirit God gave us does not make us timid, but gives us power, love and self-discipline. **2 Timothy 1:7**

DEVOTIONAL

Practicing self-control often means choosing what truly enriches our lives over fleeting satisfaction.

What areas in your life do you feel you struggle the most with self-control? How would your daily experiences change if you practiced a little more self-discipline?

PRAYER

Dear God, thank you for being our guide and strength. Help us to grow in self-control and make choices that honor You and build a better version of ourselves every day.

Self-control is the unseen muscle that strengthens our character.

OWNING MY MISTAKES

For all have sinned and fall short of the glory of God. **Romans 3:23**

DEVOTIONAL

This gentle reminder from the Apostle Paul resonates deeply, reminding us that everyone, regardless of age, carries imperfections. Owning our mistakes opens the door to growth and deeper connections with others, building a foundation of trust and respect.

What does it feel like when you know you've messed up? How do you usually respond—do you own it, or do you hide from it?

PRAYER

God, help me to see my mistakes as chances to learn and grow. Give me courage to own them and the wisdom to make things right. Thank You for loving me even when I stumble.

Owning my mistakes creates space for growth and true strength.

CHOOSING HUMILITY

Do nothing out of selfish ambition or vain conceit. Rather, in humility value others above yourselves, not looking to your own interests but each of you to the interests of the others. **Philippians 2:3-4**

DEVOTIONAL

This verse encourages us to weave humility into the fabric of our everyday interactions, offering a gentle reminder that our worth is magnified when we uplift others above our own desires. Choosing humility isn't a sign of weakness; it opens doors to stronger connections and teamwork.

What does humility look like in your life, and how can you practice it in your relationships with friends, family, and even yourself?

PRAYER

Dear God, help me to walk in humility today. Remind me that true strength is found in serving others and that I can be a light in this world by putting others before myself.

Humility opens the door to understanding and connection, while pride builds walls that isolate us.

WALKING THE TALK

In the same way, let your light shine before others, that they may see your good deeds and glorify your Father in heaven. **Matthew 5:16**

DEVOTIONAL

Being a light in someone else's life often shines brighter than any achievement we can claim for ourselves.

What does it really mean for you to live out your values every day? Can you think of a recent moment where your actions aligned with what you believe, or perhaps a time when they didn't?

PRAYER

Dear God, help me to live authentically and let my actions reflect my faith. Give me the strength to be true to myself and to You in every situation. Amen.

True integrity shines brightest when no one is watching.

GROWING IN GRIT

Blessed is the one who perseveres under trial because, having stood the test, that person will receive the crown of life that the Lord has promised to those who love him. **James 1:12**

DEVOTIONAL

Grit is not merely about talent but the courage to rise after a fall and push through adversity, transforming challenges into stepping stones for growth.

What challenges have you faced lately that tested your determination? How did you respond, and what can you learn from it to grow stronger?

PRAYER

Dear God, help me to embrace challenges that come my way. Give me the strength and resilience to keep pushing forward, even when things get tough.

Grit is not just about toughness; it's about having the passion and perseverance to pursue your goals despite the obstacles.

EVERY CHOICE MATTERS

If any of you lacks wisdom, you should ask God, who gives generously to all without finding fault, and it will be given to you. **James 1:5**

DEVOTIONAL

Every choice we make, big or small, has the power to shape our lives and the lives of those around us.

What choices are you making today that could impact your future tomorrow? Think about the little decisions—how you treat your friends, the time spent on your phone, or the way you respond to challenges. What does each choice reflect about who you want to be?

PRAYER

Dear God, help me to recognize the importance of my choices. Give me wisdom and strength to make decisions that align with my values and dreams. Thank you for guiding me every step of the way.

Every choice is a seed planted in the garden of your life.

JANUARY 22

LEARNING FROM FAILURE

For though the righteous fall seven times, they rise again, but the wicked stumble when calamity strikes. **Proverbs 24:16**

DEVOTIONAL

Even in our failures, we uncover valuable lessons that pave the way to our successes.

What's a recent failure you've faced, and what did it teach you about yourself or your goals? How can you use that lesson to grow moving forward?

PRAYER

Dear God, thank you for always being there for us, even when we stumble. Help me to embrace my failures as stepping stones on my journey, and give me the strength to learn and grow from them.

Failure is not the end; it's a lesson wrapped in a challenge.

JANUARY 23

SAYING NO WITH CONFIDENCE

Whatever you do, work at it with all your heart, as working for the Lord, not for human masters. **Colossians 3:23**

DEVOTIONAL

Life Lesson Standing tall in one's decisions can illuminate the path to true friendships and inner strength.

What are some situations in your life where saying no feels hard, but you know it's the right choice? How can remembering your values help you navigate those moments?

PRAYER

Dear God, help me to find the courage to say no when I need to. Remind me that I am strong enough to stand up for what is right and true. Thank you for always being by my side.

Confidence in saying no is just as important as knowing when to say yes.

JANUARY 24

BEING A LEADER, NOT A FOLLOWER

Do not conform to the pattern of this world, but be transformed by the renewing of your mind. Then you will be able to test and approve what God's will is—his good, pleasing and perfect will. **Romans 12:2**

DEVOTIONAL

Choosing to lead means standing firm in your values, even when it's tough.

What does it mean for you to be a leader in your own life? Are there situations where you feel you're just going along with what others want instead of stepping up and making your own choices?

PRAYER

Dear God, help me to find the courage and strength to stand firm in my beliefs and lead by example. Guide me in making choices that honor You and inspire others. May I be a light in my friendships and community, showing others the way to love and truth.

True leaders are those who inspire others to be their best selves.

MAKING WISE FRIENDS

You adulterous people, don't you know that friendship with the world means enmity against God? Therefore, anyone who chooses to be a friend of the world becomes an enemy of God. **James 4:4**

DEVOTIONAL

Choosing friends who support your journey and share your values can lead you to a more fulfilling and authentic life.

What qualities do you look for in a friend, and how do those qualities reflect who you are and want to become? Consider how your friends influence your choices and mindset.

PRAYER

Dear God, help me to seek friendships that uplift and inspire. Guide me to choose companions who challenge me to grow and reflect Your love. Thank You for the gift of friendship.

Wise friends lead you to become the best version of yourself.

JANUARY 26

MEDIA & MUSIC INFLUENCE

Above all else, guard your heart, for everything you do flows from it.
Proverbs 4:23

DEVOTIONAL

Choose music and media that inspire you and lead you toward your best self.
What songs or shows have been influencing how you see yourself and the world around you? Are there any messages that you resonate with, and how do those messages shape your thoughts and actions?

PRAYER

God, help me to be mindful of the media I consume and the music I listen to. Guide me to embrace messages that uplift my spirit and reflect your truth. May I find strength and wisdom in the choices I make.

Your mind is a garden; what you plant there will grow.

WHEN THINGS DON'T GO MY WAY

Many are the plans in a person's heart, but it is the Lord's purpose that prevails. **Proverbs 19:21**

DEVOTIONAL

When life throws you curveballs, remember that there's often a purpose behind the disappointment, and you might find something even greater along the way.

What do you feel when things don't go your way, and how do you usually respond in those moments? Can you think of a time when a setback led to something good in your life later on?

PRAYER

Dear God, help me to trust you when life doesn't go as planned. Give me strength to see the bigger picture and peace in the waiting. Amen.

Sometimes the detours take us to the most beautiful destinations.

JANUARY 28

THINKING BEFORE I POST

But test them all; hold on to what is good. **1 Thessalonians 5:21**

DEVOTIONAL

Before you hit "post," take a moment to think about how your words may impact others and remember to choose kindness. Think about this—the internet is like a giant playground where everything we do can be seen by everyone. Before you post that epic meme or share that wild opinion, remember this verse. It's not just about saying what you think; it's about making sure what you say reflects who you really are and what you believe in.

What are the feelings and thoughts that come to your mind when you think about the posts you've shared online? Do you take a moment to consider how they might affect others or yourself, both now and in the future?

PRAYER

Dear God, help me to pause and reflect before I post. Teach me the wisdom to think of how my words can uplift and impact those around me. Guide my heart and mind in using social media for good.

Words can build bridges, but they can also burn them.

JANUARY 29

CHOOSING THE HARD RIGHT

Do not be deceived: God cannot be mocked. A man reaps what he sows.
Galatians 6:7

DEVOTIONAL

Sometimes it feels like we can get away with making easy choices, but the truth is, the decisions we make have long-term consequences. It's like planting seeds; what we choose to nurture will eventually grow. Choosing the hard right over the easy wrong shapes your character and leads you to a life filled with purpose and integrity.

What does "choosing the hard right" mean for you in your everyday life? Can you think of a situation where you felt tempted to take the easy path instead? How might choosing the harder choice lead to real growth or a stronger character?

PRAYER

God, help me to find the courage to choose the hard right, even when it's tough. Give me strength when I feel weak and wisdom to know the way. Thank you for always guiding me on the right path.

Choosing the hard right builds the strength of character that shapes who you are.

JANUARY 30

GUARDING WHAT I WATCH

Finally, brothers and sisters, whatever is true, whatever is noble, whatever is right, whatever is pure, whatever is lovely, whatever is admirable—if anything is excellent or praiseworthy—think about such things.
Philippians 4:8

DEVOTIONAL

Think of it like this: if you wouldn't watch it with your little brother or sister around, maybe you shouldn't be watching it at all. What we choose to watch shapes our thoughts and actions, so it's crucial to guard that content wisely.

What kind of messages am I allowing into my mind through what I watch, and how do they shape my thoughts and actions?

PRAYER

Dear God, help me to be mindful of what I choose to watch. Guide my heart and mind to focus on things that uplift me and draw me closer to You. Amen.

Your eyes are windows to your soul; what you let in can either light your path or lead you astray.

MANAGING ANGER

Whoever is patient has great understanding, but one who is quick-tempered displays folly. **Proverbs 14:29**

DEVOTIONAL
Don't let anger control you; be in charge of your reactions and choose to rise above.

What situations make you feel most angry? How do you typically respond in those moments?

PRAYER
God, help me to pause before I react in anger. Teach me to handle my feelings with grace and understanding, just like You would. Amen.

Anger is a feeling; how we respond to it is a choice.

FEBRUARY 1

WHEN I FEEL ALONE

The Lord is close to the brokenhearted and saves those who are crushed in spirit. **Psalm 34:18**

DEVOTIONAL

No matter how isolated you feel, remember that opening up to others can reveal the support waiting just around the corner.

When was the last time you felt truly alone? How did you handle that moment, and were there ways you found support or comfort?

PRAYER

Dear God, when I feel isolated or overlooked, remind me that You are always by my side. Help me to reach out to those who care about me and to seek your presence in my life. Amen.

You are never truly alone; the strength you seek often lies within and beside you.

FEBRUARY 2

DEALING WITH STRESS

Do not be anxious about anything, but in every situation, by prayer and petition, with thanksgiving, present your requests to God. And the peace of God, which transcends all understanding, will guard your hearts and your minds in Christ Jesus. **Philippians 4:6-7**

DEVOTIONAL

Stress is tough, but leaning on God for support can help clear your mind and lift your burdens.

What are some stressors in your life right now, and how do they make you feel? Can you identify ways to tackle them, or perhaps share them with someone who cares?

PRAYER

Dear God, help me find peace in the midst of my stress. Guide me as I navigate challenges and remind me that I am never alone.

Stress is like a storm; it can be overwhelming, but it always passes.

GOD IN MY ANXIETY

Therefore do not worry about tomorrow, for tomorrow will worry about itself. Each day has enough trouble of its own. **Matthew 6:34**

DEVOTIONAL

Remember, when anxiety hits, focus on what you can do today and trust that God has your back for tomorrow.

What are the things that fill your heart and mind with worry, and how can you invite God into those moments?

PRAYER

Dear God, help me to see that I am never alone in my struggles. I ask for your peace to calm my thoughts and your strength to face my fears.

Even in the chaos of anxiety, God whispers peace into our hearts.

HANDLING DISAPPOINTMENT

Hope deferred makes the heart sick, but a longing fulfilled is a tree of life. **Proverbs 13:12**

DEVOTIONAL

Disappointment doesn't define you; how you respond to it shows your true character.

What disappointments have you faced lately, and how did you handle them? Can you think of a time when a setback turned into something better than you expected?

PRAYER

Dear God, help me to see beyond my disappointments and trust that You have a plan for my life. Give me strength to move forward and wisdom to learn from every situation. Amen.

Disappointment is just a stepping stone on the path to something greater.

FIGHTING NEGATIVE THOUGHTS

For he is the kind of person who is always thinking about the cost. "Eat and drink," he says to you, but his heart is not with you. **Proverbs 23:7**

DEVOTIONAL
Don't let negative thoughts define you; choose to focus on the qualities that make you unique and worthy.

What are some negative thoughts that creep into your mind, and how do they affect your day-to-day life?

PRAYER
Dear God, help me to recognize the negative thoughts that invade my mind. Give me the strength to push them away and fill my heart with positivity and hope. Amen.

Your thoughts are like clouds—they may come and go, but you have the power to choose what the weather in your mind looks like.

FEBRUARY 6

BUILDING CONFIDENCE

*I praise you because I am fearfully and wonderfully made; your works are wonderful, I know that full well. **Psalm 139:14***

DEVOTIONAL
You are built with unique strengths, so embrace who you are and have faith in the journey ahead.

What's one thing you're afraid to try because you doubt your abilities? How would your life change if you took that leap and gave it a shot?

PRAYER
God, thank You for believing in me, even when I struggle to believe in myself. Help me to trust in the gifts You've given me and to step out with courage. Fill me with confidence as I take steps toward my dreams.

Confidence is not about being perfect; it's about believing that you are enough just as you are.

WHEN I'M SAD

"I have told you these things, so that in me you may have peace. In this world you will have trouble. But take heart! I have overcome the world."
John 16:33

DEVOTIONAL

It's okay to feel sad sometimes; talking it out can bring unexpected support and understanding.

What are some things that make you feel sad, and how do you usually respond to that feeling? Have you considered what God might be saying to you in those moments?

PRAYER

God, thank You for always being there for me, especially when I feel sad. Help me to remember that it's okay to feel this way and guide me through my emotions with Your love. Amen.

Sadness is not a weakness; it's an authentic part of being human and a step towards healing.

FEBRUARY 8

FINDING PEACE

Peace I leave with you; my peace I give you. I do not give to you as the world gives. Do not let your hearts be troubled and do not be afraid.
John 14:27

DEVOTIONAL

When life feels overwhelming, it's okay to step back, breathe, and find peace in the quiet moments.

What does peace mean to you, and when was the last time you felt it in your heart? Think about a time when stress or chaos surrounded you. How did you cope, and what would it look like to invite God's peace into similar moments in the future?

PRAYER

God, may Your peace wash over me like a gentle wave, calming my worries and fears. Help me to find stillness in the chaos of my life and seek Your presence in every moment. Amen.

Peace isn't the absence of noise; it's the presence of a quiet heart.

LETTING GO OF CONTROL

Trust in the Lord with all your heart and lean not on your own understanding; in all your ways submit to him, and he will make your paths straight. **Proverbs 3:5-6**

DEVOTIONAL

Letting go of control can lead you to unexpected victories and a deeper understanding of the game of life.

What areas of your life are you holding onto too tightly, and how do you think letting go could help you grow?

PRAYER

God, help me to trust you with the things I can't control. Teach me to release my grip and embrace the peace that comes from relying on your strength.

Sometimes, the bravest thing you can do is simply surrender.

BEING A LOYAL FRIEND

A friend loves at all times, and a brother is born for a time of adversity.
Proverbs 17:17

DEVOTIONAL

Remember, being a loyal friend means sticking with your buddies during the good times and bad, showing them they're never alone in their struggles.

What does being a loyal friend mean to you, and how can you show that loyalty in your relationships each day? Think about specific moments where you can step up for someone you care about.

PRAYER

Dear God, help me to be a friend who stands by others with love and integrity. Teach me how to support my friends and be there for them in both good times and bad.

Loyalty isn't just about being there; it's about showing up even when it's tough.

FORGIVING OTHERS

For if you forgive other people when they sin against you, your heavenly Father will also forgive you. But if you do not forgive others their sins, your Father will not forgive your sins. **Matthew 6:14-15**

DEVOTIONAL

Forgiving others frees you from carrying around bitterness and lets you heal both yourself and your relationships.

What comes to mind when you think about someone who has hurt you? Can you recall a time when you found it hard to forgive someone? How might your life change if you decided to let go of that hurt?

PRAYER

Dear God, help me to open my heart and let go of grudges. Teach me the power of forgiveness and how it can free me from the past. Amen.

Forgiveness isn't just for them; it's for you, too.

WHEN FRIENDS HURT YOU

If an enemy were insulting me, I could endure it; if a foe were rising against me, I could hide. But it is you, a man like myself, my companion, my close friend, with whom I once enjoyed sweet fellowship at the house of God, as we walked about among the worshipers. **Psalm 55:12-14**

DEVOTIONAL

Remember, it's okay to feel pain from betrayal, but trust that real friends will stand by you and that forgiveness can lead to healing.

What do you feel when a friend lets you down or hurts you? How do you typically respond, and do you think there's a better way to handle it?

PRAYER

God, please help me find peace when I'm hurt by my friends. Teach me to forgive and understand, and remind me that I am never alone in my struggles. Amen.

Friendship is a mirror that reflects both the beauty and the brokenness of our hearts.

RESPECTING MY PARENTS

Children, obey your parents in the Lord, for this is right. "Honor your father and mother"—which is the first commandment with a promise— "so that it may go well with you and that you may enjoy long life on the earth."
Ephesians 6:1-3

DEVOTIONAL
Respecting your parents isn't just about following rules;
it's about building strong connections that last a lifetime.

What is one way you can show your parents respect this week, even if you don't always agree with them? How might this choice improve your relationship with them?

PRAYER
Dear God, thank you for the parents you have given me. Help me to see their love and guidance, and give me the strength to respect them, even when it's hard.

Respecting your parents is not just about obedience;
it's about valuing their experience and love.

SIBLING STRUGGLES

Therefore encourage one another and build each other up, just as in fact you are doing. **1 Thessalonians 5:11**

DEVOTIONAL
In every sibling struggle, remember that your words have the power to either tear down or build up the relationship you share.

What are some ways you and your sibling could work together better, despite your differences? How can you show love and understanding in moments of conflict?

PRAYER
God, help me to see my sibling as a gift rather than a challenge. Teach me to show patience and kindness, even when things get tough. Amen.

Every struggle with a sibling can be a step toward deeper love and understanding.

FEBRUARY 15

BEING A PEACEMAKER

Blessed are the peacemakers, for they will be called children of God.
Matthew 5:9

DEVOTIONAL
When you choose to be a peacemaker, you build bridges instead of walls,
fostering stronger connections in your life.

*What does it look like for you to be a peacemaker in your friendships and
school life? Are there moments when you feel called to step in and help
others find peace?*

PRAYER
God, help me to be a source of peace. Give me the courage to step
into conflict with love and understanding, guiding my friends toward
unity and kindness.

Being a peacemaker is about choosing to build bridges instead of walls.

FEBRUARY 16

CHOOSING FRIENDS WISELY

Do not be misled: "Bad company corrupts good character."
1 Corinthians 15:33

DEVOTIONAL
Choose friends who lift you up and drive you to greatness,
not those who pull you down.

*What qualities do you look for in a friend, and how do those choices reflect
your own values and dreams? Think about a time when a friend's influence
changed your perspective or decisions.*

PRAYER
Dear God, help me to see the value of choosing friends who uplift
and inspire me. Give me the wisdom to recognize those who truly
care and want the best for me. Amen.

Your friendships shape your future; choose those who light the path ahead.

WHEN I FEEL LEFT OUT

Keep your lives free from the love of money and be content with what you have, because God has said, "Never will I leave you; never will I forsake you."
Hebrews 13:5

DEVOTIONAL

When you feel left out, remember that your true friends—and God—are always with you, ready to remind you of your worth.

When was the last time you felt left out? How did it make you feel, and what did you do about it?

PRAYER

Dear God, help me remember that even when I feel left out, I am never alone. Surround me with your love and guide me through this feeling. Thank you for always being there for me.

Feeling left out is normal, but it's also a reminder that you belong to something bigger—God's family.

FEBRUARY 18

GODLY INFLUENCE

Do everything without grumbling or arguing, so that you may become blameless and pure, "children of God without fault in a warped and crooked generation." Then you will shine among them like stars in the sky.
Philippians 2:14-15

DEVOTIONAL

Influencing others positively can turn a simple moment into a lasting memory and help you shine in your own unique way.

What are some ways you can positively influence your friends and those around you, even in small actions or words each day?

PRAYER

God, help me to be a light in the lives of others. Give me the courage to stand for what is right and inspire those around me to do the same. Amen.

Your influence can spark change, even in the smallest moments.

FRIENDSHIP BREAKUPS

My command is this: Love each other as I have loved you. **John 15:12**

DEVOTIONAL
Friendships may come and go, but each one teaches us something important about ourselves and others.

What does friendship mean to you, and how do you feel when a friendship changes or ends? Have you ever considered how letting go can also be a way to grow and discover new connections?

PRAYER
Dear God, help me navigate the challenging moments of friendship breakups. Give me strength to let go of what no longer serves me and guide me towards new and uplifting relationships.

Sometimes, letting go is the first step to finding the right people who truly support you.

HOW TO PRAY

Rejoice always, pray continually, give thanks in all circumstances; for this is God's will for you in Christ Jesus. **1 Thessalonians 5:16-18**

DEVOTIONAL
Prayer isn't about saying the right words; it's about being real with God and opening your heart to Him.

What does prayer mean to you, and how can you make it a regular part of your life? Can you think of a moment when you felt close to God or needed His guidance?

PRAYER
Dear God, thank You for always being there for me. Help me to open my heart in prayer and listen for Your voice in my life. Guide me as I grow and learn more about You.

Prayer is not just talking to God, it's also listening to what He has to say.

READING THE BIBLE DAILY

Your word is a lamp for my feet, a light on my path. **Psalm 119:105**

DEVOTIONAL

Reading the Bible daily isn't just about the words on the page; it's about letting them light your way through life's challenges.

What would change in your life if you made it a habit to read the Bible every day? How might it help you face your challenges or strengthen your dreams?

PRAYER

Dear God, thank you for your Word that guides us. Help me to make time each day to connect with you through the Bible, so I can grow and understand you better.

Make space for God's Word in your life, and it will help you see things more clearly.

MEMORIZING GOD'S WORD

To the Jews who had believed him, Jesus said, "If you hold to my teaching, you are really my disciples. Then you will know the truth, and the truth will set you free." **John 8:31-32**

DEVOTIONAL

When you tuck God's Word into your heart and mind, it becomes your playbook for life, guiding you when things get tough.

What verse or passage do you think could help guide you through a tough situation this week? How might committing that to memory change your perspective?

PRAYER

God, help me to hide your Word in my heart, so I can carry your truth with me wherever I go. Teach me to find strength and guidance in Scripture. Amen.

Memorizing God's Word is like having a secret weapon ready for life's battles.

WORSHIP WITH MY LIFE

Worship the Lord with gladness; come before him with joyful songs.
Psalm 100:2

DEVOTIONAL
Worship isn't just about what happens in church; it's about how you live every day with purpose and joy, reflecting your faith in all that you do.

What does it mean for you to worship God not just on Sundays, but every day through your choices, friendships, and passions? How can you actively show that your love for Him transcends just words?

PRAYER
Dear God, help me to see the ways I can honor You in my daily life. May my actions reflect Your love and light so that others can see You through me. Amen.

Worship is not just about songs we sing; it's the life we live every day.

WHAT IS QUIET TIME?

This is what the Sovereign Lord, the Holy One of Israel, says: "In repentance and rest is your salvation, in quietness and trust is your strength, but you would have none of it. **Isaiah 30:15**

DEVOTIONAL
Your quiet time is where you find strength, clarity, and peace in a world full of noise.

What does quiet time mean to you, and how can taking a few moments for yourself each day deepen your relationship with God? Can you find a spot where you can disconnect from the noise and let your mind settle?

PRAYER
Dear God, thank You for inviting us into quiet moments with You. Help me to recognize the importance of these times and to seek Your presence in the stillness. Amen.

Quiet time is where you discover the loudest voice in the silence: God.

TRUSTING GOD'S TIMING

Let perseverance finish its work so that you may be mature and complete, not lacking anything. **James 1:4**

DEVOTIONAL

Trusting God's timing might feel tough, but remember that waiting can lead to growth and strength you didn't know you needed.

What are some areas in your life where you find it hard to trust that God is working things out in His perfect timing? How can you shift your focus to that trust today?

PRAYER

Dear God, help me to see beyond my immediate desires and to trust that Your timing is perfect. Give me patience and peace as I wait for Your plans to unfold in my life.

Patience isn't just waiting; it's keeping a good attitude while waiting.

FEBRUARY 26

ASKING GOD FOR GUIDANCE

Whether you turn to the right or to the left, your ears will hear a voice behind you, saying, "This is the way; walk in it." **Isaiah 30:21**

DEVOTIONAL

When you seek God's advice in times of confusion, He will help you find the right direction just like He did for Jake.

What's something in your life right now where you feel like you could really use God's guidance? How can you take a moment today to lay that concern before Him?

PRAYER

Dear God, thank You for always being there for me. Help me to seek your wisdom and listen to your voice as I navigate my challenges. Guide my steps each day.

God's guidance is like a compass; trust it to show you the right path, even when the way seems unclear.

LISTENING TO GOD

For the Lord gives wisdom; from his mouth come knowledge and understanding. **Proverbs 2:6**

DEVOTIONAL

Trust that taking a moment to listen can lead you to make choices that feel right for you.

What are some ways you feel God might be trying to speak to you right now, and are you taking the time to really listen?

PRAYER

Dear God, help me to quiet my mind and heart so I can hear Your voice clearly. Guide me in my daily choices and lead me closer to you. Thank You for always being there.

Listening to God is not just about hearing; it's about responding.

FEBRUARY 28

FASTING: WHAT AND WHY?

"When you fast, do not look somber as the hypocrites do, for they disfigure their faces to show others they are fasting. Truly I tell you, they have received their reward in full. But when you fast, put oil on your head and wash your face, so that it will not be obvious to others that you are fasting, but only to your Father, who is unseen; and your Father, who sees what is done in secret, will reward you." *Matthew 6:16-18*

DEVOTIONAL

Fasting isn't just about skipping meals; it's about making space for God and deepening your connection with Him.

What do you think fasting means to you personally? Can you think of a time when giving something up helped you focus more on what really matters in your life?

PRAYER

God, thank you for the opportunity to draw closer to you through fasting. Help me understand what to focus on during this time and guide me in my journey. Amen.

Fasting is not just about giving up food; it's a chance to clear the clutter and tune into what truly matters.

MARCH 1

FAITH OVER FEELINGS

Now faith is confidence in what we hope for and assurance about what we do not see. **Hebrews 11:1**

DEVOTIONAL

The key takeaway is that your feelings can fluctuate, but your faith—whether in yourself, your support system, or something greater—remains a solid foundation to build your life upon.

What do you feel right now that might be overshadowing your faith? How can you choose to trust God more than your emotions at this moment?

PRAYER

Dear God, help me to remember that my feelings can change, but your love never does. Help me to lean on you more than my emotions and guide me in trusting your plan for my life.

Faith is not about feeling, but about believing in what is true.

MARCH 2

STANDING UP FOR WHAT'S RIGHT

Do not be overcome by evil, but overcome evil with good. **Romans 12:21**

DEVOTIONAL

Sometimes, taking a stand for what is right might feel uncomfortable, but it can create a wave of change.

What are some situations in your life where you feel you need to stand up for what's right, even if it's difficult? How can you prepare yourself to take that stand when the time comes?

PRAYER

Dear God, help me to be courageous in standing up for what's right. Fill my heart with strength and wisdom to make choices that reflect Your love and truth in my life. Amen.

True strength is not just about physical power; it's about having the courage to do the right thing when it matters most.

BEING DIFFERENT FOR A REASON

But you are a chosen people, a royal priesthood, a holy nation, God's special possession, that you may declare the praises of him who called you out of darkness into his wonderful light. **1 Peter 2:9**

DEVOTIONAL

Being different isn't a weakness but a strength that can inspire others and light your path in life.

What makes you feel different from those around you? How can that uniqueness be a strength in your life and your relationships?

PRAYER

Dear God, thank You for creating me uniquely. Help me to embrace my differences and use them for Your glory. Guide me to understand that being different is a part of Your perfect plan for my life.

Being different isn't a hurdle; it's a powerful gift waiting to be unwrapped.

MARCH 4

SHARING MY FAITH

So do not be ashamed of the testimony about our Lord or of me his prisoner. Rather, join with me in suffering for the gospel, by the power of God. **2 Timothy 1:8**

DEVOTIONAL

Sharing your faith can turn moments of loneliness into powerful connections that uplift both you and others.

What does sharing your faith look like in your everyday life, and who are the people around you that you could talk to about it this week?

PRAYER

Dear God, help me to see the opportunities You place in my path to share Your love. Give me the courage and wisdom to speak about my faith with those around me. Amen.

Faith shared is faith multiplied.

MARCH 5

LEADING BY EXAMPLE

Don't let anyone look down on you because you are young, but set an example for the believers in speech, in conduct, in love, in faith and in purity.
1 Timothy 4:12

DEVOTIONAL

The way you live your life today can inspire those around you to be better tomorrow.

What does it mean for you to be a leader in your circle of friends or family? How can your actions inspire others to be better versions of themselves?

PRAYER

God, thank you for the unique role you've given me among my friends. Help me to lead by example, showing kindness and strength in every situation I face.

Your actions speak so loudly that others may never hear your words.

MARCH 6

FAITH IN HARD MOMENTS

So do not fear, for I am with you; do not be dismayed, for I am your God. I will strengthen you and help you; I will uphold you with my righteous right hand. **Isaiah 41:10**

DEVOTIONAL

When life gets tough, turning to God in prayer can bring you the strength you need to face challenges head-on.

What challenges are you facing right now that make it hard to trust that everything will work out? How can you lean on your faith during these tough times?

PRAYER

God, I ask that you bring peace to my heart in times of struggle. Help me to trust in Your plan and find strength in my faith. Let me see the light in dark moments.

Even in the hardest moments, faith is the strength that carries us through.

WHEN I'M THE ONLY CHRISTIAN

Even though I walk through the darkest valley, I will fear no evil, for you are with me; your rod and your staff, they comfort me. **Psalm 23:4**

DEVOTIONAL

Standing alone for your faith can be tough, but it strengthens your character and shows true courage.

When you find yourself surrounded by friends or peers who don't share your faith, how do you feel? Do you find it challenging to stand up for what you believe in, or do you feel empowered to be a light in that situation?

PRAYER

Dear God, thank you for being with me in all situations. Help me to stand strong in my faith, especially when I'm the only one who believes. Give me courage and wisdom to shine your light in my world.

Being the only Christian can feel lonely, but it's also an opportunity to stand out and make a difference.

SPEAKING TRUTH WITH KINDNESS

A gentle answer turns away wrath, but a harsh word stirs up anger.
Proverbs 15:1

DEVOTIONAL

Always remember that how you say something can be just as important as what you say; speaking truth with kindness can lead to better understanding and respect.

What does it mean to you to speak the truth kindly? Can you think of a time when you had to share something honest but found a way to do it without hurting someone's feelings? How did it make you feel afterward?

PRAYER

Dear God, help me to speak the truth with kindness. Teach me to choose my words wisely so that I can uplift others while staying true to myself.
Amen.

Grace and truth can walk hand in hand.

CONFIDENCE THROUGH CHRIST

Cast all your anxiety on him because he cares for you. **1 Peter 5:7**

DEVOTIONAL

No matter where you stand in your abilities or insecurities, lean on Christ, and you'll find confidence that transforms your fears into strength.

What situations in your life make you feel unsure of yourself? How might knowing that Christ believes in you change your perspective in those moments?

PRAYER

Dear God, thank You for the strength and confidence You offer through Your love. Help me to embrace my true identity in Christ and to trust in Your plan, no matter what challenges I face.

Confidence isn't about being perfect; it's about knowing you're enough just as you are.

RISKING COMFORT FOR PURPOSE

Do not merely listen to the word, and so deceive yourselves. Do what it says. **James 1:22**

DEVOTIONAL

Sometimes, we have to let go of our comfort to discover who we're meant to be and what we can achieve. Embrace the uncomfortable moments; they are often where purpose and growth begin.

What are some comforts in your life that you might need to set aside in order to chase a greater purpose? Think about how you can take a step towards that this week.

PRAYER

God, help me to step outside of my comfort zone and trust in Your plans for me. Give me the courage to pursue my purpose, even when it feels challenging. Amen.

True growth happens outside of your comfort zone.

FAITH IN PUBLIC

Let us hold unswervingly to the hope we profess, for he who promised is faithful. **Hebrews 10:23**

DEVOTIONAL

Having faith in public isn't just about grand gestures; it's often the small, brave choices to show love and compassion that matter most.

What does it mean for you to live out your faith in front of your friends at school or in sports? How do you balance your beliefs with the expectations around you?

PRAYER

Dear God, help me to stand strong in my faith, even when it feels tough. Give me courage to shine Your light in my daily life and to be a true reflection of Your love to others.

True faith shines brightest in the places where it's most challenged.

MARCH 12

WHY AM I HERE?

Now you are the body of Christ, and each one of you is a part of it. **1 Corinthians 12:27**

DEVOTIONAL

You are valuable and have a unique role to play in the world; never underestimate your worth.

What do you think your unique talents and passions say about your purpose in life? How can you take steps today to explore and embrace that purpose?

PRAYER

Dear God, thank You for creating me with a purpose. Help me to discover and embrace the gifts You've given me, and to use them to make a positive impact in the world around me.

Your purpose is written in the talents you've been given and the passions that ignite your heart.

WHAT GOD SAYS ABOUT SUCCESS

Brothers and sisters, I do not consider myself yet to have taken hold of it. But one thing I do: Forgetting what is behind and straining toward what is ahead, I press on toward the goal to win the prize for which God has called me heavenward in Christ Jesus. **Philippians 3:13-14**

DEVOTIONAL

Success isn't measured solely by winning; it's about the effort you put in and how you grow from the process.

What does success look like to you, and how does it fit into the bigger picture of your life and faith? Is it about grades, sports, or something deeper?

PRAYER

God, thank you for guiding me on my journey. Help me to seek true success in my life, shaped by your love and purpose. Lead me to understand that my worth is defined by You, not by my achievements.

Success is not measured by the world's standards,
but by the heart's alignment with God's purpose.

MARCH 14

DISCOVERING MY GIFTS

There are different kinds of gifts, but the same Spirit distributes them. There are different kinds of service, but the same Lord. There are different kinds of working, but in all of them and in everyone it is the same God at work.
1 Corinthians 12:4-6

DEVOTIONAL

Your gifts can shine brighter and impact others when you dare to share them.

What talents or interests do you have that bring you joy or excitement? How might these gifts offer purpose to your life, and how can you share them with others?

PRAYER

Dear God, thank you for the unique gifts you've placed within me. Help me to recognize and embrace them, using them to glorify You and serve those around me.

Your gifts are not just for you; they are meant to shine and inspire others.

MARCH 15

DREAMING BIG WITH GOD

See, I am doing a new thing! Now it springs up; do you not perceive it?
I am making a way in the wilderness and streams in the wasteland.
Isaiah 43:19

DEVOTIONAL
Don't settle for small dreams; trust that God has something incredible
for you that might be just around the corner.

What big dreams do you have right now, and how can you see God
being a part of making those dreams come true?

PRAYER
God, thank you for the dreams You place in our hearts. Help me to trust in
Your plan and to chase after those dreams with courage and faith. Amen.

With God, your dreams aren't just hopes; they're stepping stones to
something greater.

MARCH 16

MAKING THE MOST OF MY YOUTH

The glory of young men is their strength, gray hair the splendor of the old.
Proverbs 20:29

DEVOTIONAL
Don't waste your youth; instead, try new things and embrace opportunities
that come your way.

What are the dreams and passions you have that you've been letting sit on
the back burner? How can you take a small step towards them today?

PRAYER
Dear God, thank you for the gift of youth and the potential that comes with it.
Help me to embrace every moment and make choices that lead me closer
to my dreams.

Your youth is a canvas; paint it with bold colors and daring strokes.

GOD HAS A PLAN

And we know that in all things God works for the good of those who love him, who have been called according to his purpose. **Romans 8:28**

DEVOTIONAL
Trust that even when things feel tough, God is at work behind the scenes, crafting a bigger narrative that leads you to your best self.

What dreams or goals do you feel God might be nudging you toward right now, and how can you take a step toward them today?

PRAYER
Dear God, thank You for having a plan for my life, even when I can't see it. Help me to trust in Your timing and take steps in faith as You lead me.

Trusting God's plan means believing that something greater is in the works, even when the path isn't clear.

WHEN I DON'T KNOW WHAT'S NEXT

I will instruct you and teach you in the way you should go; I will counsel you with my loving eye on you. **Psalm 32:8**

DEVOTIONAL
Sometimes, it's okay not to have a plan; just take the next step and trust that you are being guided.

What are some things in your life right now that feel uncertain, and how can you approach them with courage rather than fear?

PRAYER
God, I'm stepping into the unknown right now. Help me find peace and strength as I trust in Your plan for my future. Guide my heart and mind amid the uncertainty.

Even when the road ahead is unclear, God's light will guide your steps.

MARCH 19

PREPARING FOR MANHOOD

Like newborn babies, crave pure spiritual milk, so that by it you may grow up in your salvation. **1 Peter 2:2**

DEVOTIONAL

Every choice you make today helps shape the man you'll become tomorrow.

What does it mean to you to be becoming a man? How do you feel about the responsibilities that come with that journey?

PRAYER

Dear God, help me to embrace the journey of growing into the man You created me to be. Guide my steps and give me the courage to face the challenges ahead. Thank You for always being by my side.

True strength lies not just in what you can lift, but in how you lift others up.

MARCH 20

SERVING OTHERS WITH MY TALENTS

Each of you should use whatever gift you have received to serve others, as faithful stewards of God's grace in its various forms. **1 Peter 4:10**

DEVOTIONAL

Think about that: everyone has something to give that only they can offer. Whether it's soccer skills, musical talent, or even just being a good listener, you've got something inside you that can make a difference. You can serve others with the unique gifts you have, and in doing so, you grow yourself too.

What unique talents or skills do you have that could be a blessing to those around you? How can you start using them to make a difference in someone else's life today?

PRAYER

Dear God, thank you for the unique gifts you've given each of us. Help me to see the opportunities around me to serve others and to share my talents with love and generosity.

Your talents were given to you to be shared, not hidden away.

MAKING EVERY DAY COUNT

There is a time for everything, and a season for every activity under the heavens. **Ecclesiastes 3:1**

DEVOTIONAL

Every day is a chance to create lasting memories, so choose wisely where you invest your time.

What small steps can you take today to ensure that your actions reflect the person you want to become? Think about what matters most to you and how you can make each moment meaningful.

PRAYER

Heavenly Father, help me to see the value in each day and inspire me to make choices that align with my dreams and purpose. Give me the courage to embrace challenges and the wisdom to appreciate the little victories. Amen.

Every day is a fresh page; what story will you write today?

GAMING & SELF-CONTROL

Like a city whose walls are broken through is a person who lacks self-control. **Proverbs 25:28**

DEVOTIONAL

When it comes to gaming, self-control isn't about missing out; it's about playing smart so you can still enjoy everything else life has to offer.

What are some ways gaming can impact your mood and decisions, and how can you find balance in both your gaming and your life outside of it? Think about your favorite games; do they ever distract you from what truly matters?

PRAYER

Dear God, help me to find balance in my life. Teach me the art of self-control, especially when I'm tempted to overindulge in gaming. May I always seek what brings glory to You.

Master your game, or your game will master you.

PHONES, LIKES, AND IDENTITY

But the Lord said to Samuel, "Do not consider his appearance or his height, for I have rejected him. The Lord does not look at the things people look at. People look at the outward appearance, but the Lord looks at the heart." **1 Samuel 16:7**

DEVOTIONAL

Your identity is not based on likes or followers; it's found in who God says you are and the real connections you build with others.

What do your online interactions say about how you see yourself? When you scroll through your feed or check your notifications, how do those moments shape your understanding of who you are?

PRAYER

Dear God, help me to see my worth beyond my phone screen. Remind me that my true identity is rooted in You and not in the likes I receive. Guide me to build relationships that reflect Your love and truth.

Your identity is found in how God sees you, not in how the world measures you.

HANDLING ONLINE TEMPTATION

"Watch and pray so that you will not fall into temptation. The spirit is willing, but the flesh is weak." **Matthew 26:41**

DEVOTIONAL

You have the power to choose your path, even in the face of online temptations; remember your values and trust your instincts.

What online temptations do you face regularly, and how do they make you feel about yourself and your values?

PRAYER

Dear God, guide me through the distractions of the online world. Help me to stay strong and focused on what truly matters in my life. Amen.

Your digital decisions shape your heart.

MARCH 25

PEER PRESSURE & GROUP CHATS

Blessed is the one who does not walk in step with the wicked or stand in the way that sinners take or sit in the company of mockers, but whose delight is in the law of the Lord, and who meditates on his law day and night.
Psalm 1:1-2

DEVOTIONAL
Stand firm in your values, even when your friends push you to do otherwise.

What voices do you hear in your group chats, and how do they influence your thoughts or actions? Can you remember a time when you felt pressure to fit in? What did you choose, and how did that choice reflect who you are?

PRAYER
God, help me to listen to Your voice above all others. Guide me in choosing friends and influences that uplift and encourage me in my walk with You. Amen.

True strength is standing firm in your belief, even when others seek to sway you.

MARCH 26

WHEN I'M JUDGED FOR BELIEVING

"Blessed are you when people insult you, persecute you and falsely say all kinds of evil against you because of me. Rejoice and be glad, because great is your reward in heaven, for in the same way they persecuted the prophets who were before you. *Matthew 5:11-12*

DEVOTIONAL
Standing firm in your beliefs might bring judgment, but it will always lead you closer to who you truly are.

What do you feel when others judge you for your beliefs? How can you turn that judgment into something that strengthens your faith and character?

PRAYER
Dear God, help me to stand firm in my beliefs even when others don't understand. Remind me that your love is greater than any judgment I may face.

Your faith can be your shield against the arrows of judgment.

CANCEL CULTURE VS. GRACE

Be kind and compassionate to one another, forgiving each other, just as in Christ God forgave you. **Ephesians 4:32**

DEVOTIONAL
When others mess up, let grace be your response instead of blame.

What does it mean to you to extend grace to someone who has messed up, especially when the world around you seems to favor canceling them instead?

PRAYER
Dear God, thank You for the grace You show us every day. Help me to see others through Your eyes and to be quick to offer forgiveness and understanding when someone stumbles.

Grace is the bridge we build instead of the wall we construct.

MARCH 28

TOXIC MASCULINITY VS. GODLY STRENGTH

Have I not commanded you? Be strong and courageous. Do not be afraid; do not be discouraged, for the Lord your God will be with you wherever you go." **Joshua 1:9**

DEVOTIONAL
Real strength comes from being true to yourself and showing compassion, not just from being tough or unfeeling.

What does it really mean to be strong? Are you influenced more by the expectations of society or by the values you believe in? Take a moment to think about how you define your strength.

PRAYER
Dear God, help me to understand true strength as You define it. Guide me to choose courage, kindness, and integrity over the pressures of the world. Amen.

Godly strength is the ability to lift others up while standing firm in your own beliefs.

SOCIAL MEDIA COMPARISON

We do not dare to classify or compare ourselves with some who commend themselves. When they measure themselves by themselves and compare themselves with themselves, they are not wise. **2 Corinthians 10:12**

DEVOTIONAL

True worth comes from embracing your own unique path, not from comparing your life to someone else's highlight reel.

What do you find yourself comparing when you scroll through social media? How does that make you feel about yourself? Take a moment to think about the people or images that spark these thoughts.

PRAYER

Dear God, help me to remember my worth comes from You, not likes or followers. Teach me to see my value beyond what I see online and guide my heart to uplift others instead of comparing.

Your true worth is not defined by the highlight reels you see online.

MARCH 30

FEELING BEHIND EVERYONE ELSE

Let your eyes look straight ahead; fix your gaze directly before you. Give careful thought to the paths for your feet and be steadfast in all your ways. Do not turn to the right or the left; keep your foot from evil. **Proverbs 4:25-27**

DEVOTIONAL

Sometimes, the most important part of your own story is taking the time to grow at your own pace, rather than worrying about what everyone else is doing.

What do you think it feels like to be on your own journey without comparing yourself to others? When you see your friends achieving milestones or successes, how does that make you feel about your own path?

PRAYER

God, help me to trust in the plan You have for my life. Remind me that it's okay to be in a different place than my friends, and give me the strength to embrace my own unique journey.

Your timeline is not someone else's; every step you take is part of your growth.

DEALING WITH BULLYING

One who has unreliable friends soon comes to ruin, but there is a friend who sticks closer than a brother. **Proverbs 18:24**

DEVOTIONAL
Standing together with good friends can help you overcome the hurtful words and actions of others.

What have you experienced or witnessed recently that made you feel like you were being judged or belittled by others? How did it affect you, and what steps can you take to rise above it?

PRAYER
Dear God, help me find strength and peace in the face of difficulty. May I embrace your love as I confront bullying, and empower me to support others who are hurting.

You have the power to rise above the pain and become stronger through it.

APRIL 1

CRUSHES AND BOUNDARIES

We love because he first loved us. **1 John 4:19**

DEVOTIONAL
Respecting boundaries not only honors others but also helps you grow in healthy relationships.

What does it feel like when you're drawn to someone special? How can you tell if those feelings are genuine, and what does it mean to set healthy boundaries in those situations?

PRAYER
Dear God, thank You for the feelings we experience when we connect with others. Help us to navigate these emotions with wisdom and kindness, and guide us in building respectful relationships.

Crushes can be exciting, but true character shows in the way we treat others and ourselves.

APRIL 2

DATING WITH RESPECT

Do everything in love. **1 Corinthians 16:14**

DEVOTIONAL
Always treat others how you'd want to be treated, because respect is the foundation of any strong relationship.

What does it mean to you to treat someone you're interested in with respect, and how can you show that in your words and actions?

PRAYER
Dear God, help me to see others through Your eyes. Teach me to communicate and act with kindness and respect in my relationships. Amen.

Respect is the foundation on which all healthy relationships are built.

WHY PURITY STILL MATTERS

*"I have the right to do anything," you say—but not everything is beneficial.
"I have the right to do anything"—but I will not be mastered by anything.*
1 Corinthians 6:12

DEVOTIONAL
Choosing purity equips you with strength and clarity for the battles ahead,
setting you up for real victory in life.

*What does purity mean to you in your daily life, and why do you think it's
important to keep that value in your relationships and choices? Consider
how it shapes your character and the way you interact with others.*

PRAYER
Dear God, help me to see the value in purity and to understand how it
impacts my life and those around me. Give me the strength to make
choices that reflect my beliefs and the courage to stand firm in them. Amen.

Purity isn't about perfection; it's about the journey of becoming who we're meant to be.

APRIL 4

GOD'S VIEW ON LOVE

*Dear friends, let us love one another, for love comes from God. Everyone
who loves has been born of God and knows God.* **1 John 4:7**

DEVOTIONAL
Love is about moving beyond our comfort zones and showing kindness,
just like God does for us every day.

*What does love mean to you, and how do you see it shaping your
relationships with your friends and family? Take a moment to think
about how God views love in your life.*

PRAYER
Dear God, thank you for loving me unconditionally. Help me understand
and share that love with others as I navigate my friendships and family
relationships.

True love is not just a feeling; it's a choice that reflects the heart of God.

APRIL 5

WHEN I FEEL REJECTED

Though my father and mother forsake me, the Lord will receive me.
Psalm 27:10

DEVOTIONAL

Don't let rejection define your worth; remember that your value isn't tied to what others think of you.

What situations make you feel rejected? How do those feelings impact your view of yourself and your relationships with others? Take a moment to reflect on these experiences and how they shape your thoughts.

PRAYER

Dear God, please help me remember that I am never truly alone, even when I feel rejected. Fill my heart with your love and guidance so I can learn to stand strong in my true identity.

You are never defined by the opinions of others.

APRIL 6

GUARDING MY HEART

Set your minds on things above, not on earthly things. **Colossians 3:2**

DEVOTIONAL

Always be mindful of where you invest your time and energy, because what you focus on shapes who you become.

What are the things that are currently influencing your thoughts and emotions? Are they drawing you closer to your goals and values, or pushing you away from them? Take a moment to examine what's in your heart and mind right now.

PRAYER

Dear God, help me to be mindful of what I let in my heart. Guide me to protect it from distractions and negativity while filling it with your love and wisdom. Thank you for always being with me.

Your heart is a garden; nurture it with what truly matters.

BEING THE RIGHT PERSON FIRST

Therefore, if anyone is in Christ, the new creation has come:
The old has gone, the new is here! **2 Corinthians 5:17**

DEVOTIONAL

This reminds us that every day is a chance to start fresh and show the world who we really are inside. Being genuine and true to yourself creates deeper connections and attracts friendships that matter.

What does it mean for you to be the person you want to attract? How can you start aligning your actions and character with the values you admire in others?

PRAYER

God, help me to focus on being the right person first. Guide my heart and actions so that I can reflect the qualities I seek in others. Lead me to build genuine relationships grounded in kindness and respect.

To be the change you wish to see in the world, start with yourself.

APRIL 8

LUST VS. LOVE

Flee from sexual immorality. All other sins a person commits are outside the body, but whoever sins sexually, sins against their own body.
1 Corinthians 6:18

DEVOTIONAL

True love is about valuing someone for who they are, not just what they can offer you in the moment.

What does love look like to you, and how is it different from the way lust makes you feel? Take a moment to think about a time when you felt genuine love for someone or something and how it compares to fleeting feelings of attraction.

PRAYER

Dear God, help me discern the difference between love and lust in my life. Guide my heart to seek genuine connections that reflect Your truth and goodness. Amen.

True love builds you up; lust only seeks to tear you down.

APRIL 9

RESPECTING GIRLS AS SISTERS

Treat younger men as brothers, older women as mothers, and younger women as sisters, with absolute purity. **1 Timothy 5:2**

DEVOTIONAL

This verse reminds us that every girl deserves to be treated with respect, just like you would treat your own family. When you respect girls as if they were your own sisters, you create an environment of support and dignity that everyone deserves.

What are some ways you can show respect to the girls in your life, treating them as sisters rather than just friends or classmates? How can you start this today?

PRAYER

Dear God, thank you for the girls in our lives who enrich our experiences. Help us to treat them with love and respect, recognizing their worth and our shared humanity. May we always be supportive and understanding towards them.

Respecting others is a reflection of how you view yourself.

APRIL 10

CHOOSING CHARACTER OVER COOLNESS

Whoever walks in integrity walks securely, but whoever takes crooked paths will be found out. **Proverbs 10:9**

DEVOTIONAL

Choosing to build your character is like choosing to wear armor against the pressures of the world; it's what makes you truly strong.

What does it mean for you to choose character over coolness in your everyday life? Can you think of specific moments when you've felt the pressure to fit in, and how did that affect your choices?

PRAYER

God, help me to be brave in choosing integrity over popularity. May my actions reflect the values I hold and inspire those around me. Let me remember that true strength comes from being real.

Real strength is choosing what's right over what's easy.

FAITH WHEN LIFE GETS BORING

Consider it pure joy, my brothers and sisters, whenever you face trials of many kinds, because you know that the testing of your faith produces perseverance. **James 1:2-3**

DEVOTIONAL

When life feels dull and unexciting, remember that your attitude can turn mundane moments into opportunities for growth and connection.

What do you do when life feels like it's stuck on repeat? Can you think of a time when you leaned on your faith to help you through a boring or uneventful season?

PRAYER

God, thank you for walking with us even in the dull moments of life. Help us to see Your hand at work and to trust in Your plan, even when every day feels the same. Fill our hearts with joy and purpose as we wait on You.

Even in the mundane, God is crafting a masterpiece.

DEALING WITH REGRET

Whoever conceals their sins does not prosper, but the one who confesses and renounces them finds mercy. **Proverbs 28:13**

DEVOTIONAL

You can't change the past, but you can learn from it and become stronger moving forward.

What is one decision you wish you could change, and what do you think you would do differently if given the chance? How can you use that experience to grow in the future?

PRAYER

Dear God, help me to let go of the weight of my regrets and to embrace your grace instead. Teach me how to learn from my past and to look forward with hope.

Regret is a teacher; it shows us what we value and guides us toward better choices.

APRIL 13

FOLLOWING CHRIST AT SCHOOL

When Jesus spoke again to the people, he said, "I am the light of the world. Whoever follows me will never walk in darkness, but will have the light of life."
John 8:12

DEVOTIONAL
Being a light at school might just mean being brave enough to include others, showing them they're not alone.

What does it mean for you to stand strong in your faith at school, even when it gets tough or lonely? Can you think of a time you felt challenged in your beliefs, and how would you respond differently now?

PRAYER
Dear God, thank you for being with me every day at school. Help me to stand firm in my faith and be a light to my friends, even when it's hard. Amen.

Walking with Christ means taking one step at a time in the hallways of life.

APRIL 14

TRUSTING GOD DURING TESTS

Commit your way to the Lord trust in him and he will do this. **Psalm 37:5**

DEVOTIONAL
Trusting God doesn't mean you won't face challenges; it means you can find peace and strength in the middle of them.

What is one challenge you're facing right now that makes it hard to trust God? How can you remind yourself of His presence during this test?

PRAYER
God, help me lean on You when times get tough. Teach me to see challenges as opportunities to grow and trust in Your plan for my life. Guide me through these moments with Your strength and love.

Trusting God is like a rock in the storm; it steadies you when everything else feels chaotic.

APRIL 15

BEING FAITHFUL IN SMALL THINGS

"Whoever can be trusted with very little can also be trusted with much, and whoever is dishonest with very little will also be dishonest with much.
Luke 16:10

DEVOTIONAL

In the small, everyday tasks, like mowing lawns or even helping out at home, you're building the foundation for bigger responsibilities and opportunities in your life. Being faithful in small things sets you up for greater things down the road.

What small responsibilities in your life can you show more faithfulness towards? How might being diligent in these areas benefit not just you, but also the people around you?

PRAYER

Lord, help me to see the value in the small things. Teach me to be faithful in my daily tasks and to honor You through my choices. Thank You for Your endless patience as I grow.

Greatness is often found in the daily details.

APRIL 16

MY IDENTITY IS NOT MY GRADES

But now, this is what the Lord says— he who created you, Jacob, he who formed you, Israel: "Do not fear, for I have redeemed you; I have summoned you by name; you are mine. **Isaiah 43:1**

DEVOTIONAL

Your grades may change from semester to semester, but your worth and identity remain constant and are rooted in who you are as a person, not what you achieve.

What does your heart tell you about who you are beyond your grades? Can you think of all the things that make you unique and valuable apart from school?

PRAYER

God, thank You for reminding me that my worth comes from You, not my grades or achievements. Help me to see and embrace my true identity as Your beloved child, filled with purpose and promise.

Your identity is shaped by who God says you are, not by numbers on a piece of paper.

CHOOSING MY BATTLES

If it is possible, as far as it depends on you, live at peace with everyone.
Romans 12:18

DEVOTIONAL

Choose your battles wisely, letting go of the small stuff to focus on what really counts in your life.

What battles are you facing right now, and how can you discern which ones are worth your energy and focus?

PRAYER

God, guide me in understanding the battles I should fight and those I should let go. Help me to choose wisely and strengthen me in the moments that matter. Thank you for your constant love and support.

Not every struggle is worth the fight; choose wisely where you stand.

SPENDING TIME WITH GOD DAILY

I love those who love me, and those who seek me find me. **Proverbs 8:17**

DEVOTIONAL

Make it a priority to spend time with God every day—think of it as your secret power-up for facing whatever comes your way.

What does spending time with God mean to you, and how can you make it a part of your daily routine?

PRAYER

Dear God, thank you for welcoming me into your presence. Help me to carve out time each day to connect with you and grow in my faith. Amen.

Time spent with God is never wasted; it's an investment in your soul.

WHEN GOD FEELS DISTANT

As the deer pants for streams of water, so my soul pants for you, my God. My soul thirsts for God, for the living God. When can I go and meet with God?
Psalm 42:1-2

DEVOTIONAL

Just because you can't feel God or see Him right now doesn't mean He isn't right beside you, waiting for you to reach out.

*What's one time when you felt God was distant from you,
and how did that affect your faith?*

PRAYER

Dear God, even when we feel alone, help us to remember Your presence is always near. Open our hearts to seek You during those tough times and fill us with reassurance of Your love.

Even in silence, God is working behind the scenes.

FAITH ISN'T ALWAYS A FEELING

For we live by faith, not by sight. **2 Corinthians 5:7**

DEVOTIONAL

Think about that for a moment. Sometimes, life feels like a video game where you're waiting for the next power-up to show you the way. But true faith encourages you to keep pushing forward, even when you can't see the finish line. Faith is about taking action, not just feeling a certain way; it's trusting what you believe even when it's hard to feel it.

What do you do when you don't feel close to God? How can you remind yourself that faith is about trusting His promises, even when your heart feels distant?

PRAYER

Dear God, thank you for always being there, even when I can't feel you. Help me to trust in your presence and promises, especially during times when my feelings are low. Amen.

Faith is often a choice, not just a feeling.

LEADING WITHOUT A TITLE

For lack of guidance a nation falls, but victory is won through many advisers. **Proverbs 11:14**

DEVOTIONAL
Even without a title, you can inspire and guide others through your actions and attitude.

What does it mean for you to lead others, even when no one has given you a title or formal position? Can you think of a time when you influenced someone positively, just by being yourself?

PRAYER
God, thank You for the potential You've placed in each of us. Help me to recognize opportunities to lead others with love and kindness, regardless of my title. Amen.

True leadership is about serving others and making a positive impact, no matter where you are.

THE POWER OF ENCOURAGEMENT

Do not let any unwholesome talk come out of your mouths, but only what is helpful for building others up according to their needs, that it may benefit those who listen. **Ephesians 4:29**

DEVOTIONAL
Your words have the power to lift someone's spirit, so choose them wisely and use them to build others up.

What are some ways you can encourage your friends today, and how does that make you feel when you lift someone else's spirits?

PRAYER
God, thank You for the gift of words that can uplift and inspire. Help me to be a source of encouragement to my friends and family, sharing Your love through my actions and words.

Your words have the power to build bridges or walls; choose to be the one who builds.

LEARNING TO WAIT

Wait for the Lord; be strong and take heart and wait for the Lord. **Psalm 27:14**

DEVOTIONAL
Sometimes waiting can feel like a waste of time, but often it's in those waiting moments where we find the greatest rewards.

What's one area in your life where you find it hardest to wait? Think about the feelings you have in those moments and how you might change your perspective.

PRAYER
Dear God, help me to embrace the waiting times in my life. Teach me patience and remind me that Your timing is perfect. Amen.

"Waiting is not wasting time; it's preparing you for what's next."

APRIL 24

WHAT REAL STRENGTH LOOKS LIKE

If you falter in a time of trouble, how small is your strength! **Proverbs 24:10**

DEVOTIONAL
Sometimes, real strength means showing up and pushing through the tough moments while helping others rise with you.

What does strength mean to you? Is it about being tough and never showing weakness, or is it something deeper that involves being true to yourself and standing up for others?

PRAYER
God, help me to understand the real meaning of strength. Show me how to be brave in my own unique way and support those around me with love and grace.

True strength is not the absence of fear but the courage to face it with integrity.

BEING KIND WHEN IT'S HARD

Those who are kind benefit themselves, but the cruel bring ruin on themselves. **Proverbs 11:17**

DEVOTIONAL

When faced with a choice between fitting in and doing the right thing, the right choice often takes the most courage.

What does kindness look like in tough situations for you? Can you think of a recent time when you found it difficult to be kind to someone? How did it make you feel?

PRAYER

Dear God, help me to be brave in choosing kindness, even when it feels hard. Guide my heart to understand others and to show compassion in every situation. Amen.

Kindness is a strength that shines brightest in the darkest moments.

APRIL 26

LETTING GOD CHANGE ME

You were taught, with regard to your former way of life, to put off your old self, which is being corrupted by its deceitful desires; to be made new in the attitude of your minds; and to put on the new self, created to be like God in true righteousness and holiness. **Ephesians 4:22-24**

DEVOTIONAL

What are some areas in your life where you feel God is calling you to grow or change? How can you take a small step toward that change today?

Letting God change you isn't about being perfect; it's about letting Him guide you to become the best version of yourself. Just like in that game, you have to be willing to step out of your comfort zone and embrace the new skills and challenges He presents. Sometimes it's tough to leave behind old habits or attitudes, but remember that the upgrade is worth it. It's not just about you; it's about who God created you to be. Don't be afraid to embrace change; it's how God molds you into someone amazing.

PRAYER

God, I open my heart to the changes you want to make in me. Help me embrace the journey and trust in your timing. Amen.

Real growth often happens in the moments when we let go and let God take the lead.

OBEYING EVEN WHEN I DON'T FEEL LIKE IT

Let us not become weary in doing good, for at the proper time we will reap a harvest if we do not give up. **Galatians 6:9**

DEVOTIONAL

Obeying and pushing through when you don't feel like it builds character and strength for the challenges ahead.

What are some specific times when you've felt like ignoring the right choice, and how did you decide to act anyway?

PRAYER

Dear God, help me to remember that obeying Your word brings true joy, even when it's hard. Give me the strength to choose what is right in my everyday life. Thank You for being with me every step of the way.

Obedience is not just about doing what's right; it's about trusting that God knows best.

GOD SEES MY EFFORT

Commit to the Lord whatever you do, and he will establish your plans.
Proverbs 16:3

DEVOTIONAL

This verse reminds us that when we turn our goals and dreams over to God, He's got our back, and He'll help us make things happen. Every time you put in effort, whether in sports, school, or relationships, remember that God sees it and values your heart behind it.

What efforts are you making in your life right now that you feel might be going unnoticed? How can you remember that God sees and values these even when others might not?

PRAYER

Dear God, thank You for recognizing the hard work I put in, even when no one else does. Help me to keep my heart focused on You as I strive to do my best.

Your efforts matter, even if no one else seems to be paying attention.

FITTING IN VS. STANDING OUT

On the contrary, we speak as those approved by God to be entrusted with the gospel. We are not trying to please people but God, who tests our hearts.
1 Thessalonians 2:4

DEVOTIONAL
Being true to yourself can create deeper connections
than trying to fit into a mold.

What does it feel like for you to try to fit in with your friends? Do you ever feel the pressure to change who you are in order to be accepted?

PRAYER
Dear God, thank you for the unique person you've created me to be. Help me to embrace my individuality and give me the courage to stand out for you in a world that often values conformity.

Being true to yourself is the highest form of bravery.

APRIL 30

FINDING REAL JOY

I have told you this so that my joy may be in you and that your joy may be complete. **John 15:11**

DEVOTIONAL
True joy isn't found in accomplishments or possessions, but in the moments we share with others and the love we give.

What brings you true happiness in your life? Is it fleeting moments or something deeper that lasts beyond the day-to-day? Take a moment to think about what really makes your heart smile.

PRAYER
God, thank you for the joy that comes from knowing you. Help me discover the true joy in my life that goes beyond what the world offers. May I find joy in every moment and share it with those around me.

Real joy is not found in things, but in the moments we cherish
and the relationships we cultivate.

WHEN I'M AFRAID OF THE FUTURE

So we say with confidence, "The Lord is my helper; I will not be afraid. What can mere mortals do to me?" **Hebrews 13:**

DEVOTIONAL
You don't have to have everything figured out right now; just focus on the next step and trust that God has a plan for you.

What fears do you have about your future, and how do those fears make you feel in the present moment? Take a moment to think about what you can do to replace those fears with hope.

PRAYER
Dear God, I come to you with my worries about tomorrow. Help me to trust in Your plan for my life and to find peace in knowing You are always with me. Amen.

Fear may cloud your vision of the future, but faith will light the path ahead.

STAYING CALM UNDER PRESSURE

Be joyful in hope, patient in affliction, faithful in prayer. **Romans 12:12**

DEVOTIONAL
In the whirlwind of life's challenges, a moment of calm can turn anxiety into action.

What do you find helps you stay calm when things get overwhelming? Have there been moments in your life where you've felt pressure building up, and how did you handle it?

PRAYER
Dear God, thank You for being a constant source of strength. Help me to remember that I can always turn to You when I feel the weight of the world around me. Grant me peace and clarity in times of stress.

Calmness is not about the absence of pressure, but the presence of peace within.

HELPING WITHOUT EXPECTING CREDIT

One person gives freely, yet gains even more; another withholds unduly, but comes to poverty. A generous person will prosper; whoever refreshes others will be refreshed. **Proverbs 11:24-25**

DEVOTIONAL

Helping others isn't about the credit you receive;
it's about the impact you make in their lives.

What would it look like for you to help someone today without waiting for recognition or a thank-you? How can you serve others quietly, knowing that your actions speak louder than any applause?

PRAYER

Dear God, help me to serve others with a joyful heart. Teach me the beauty of giving without expecting anything in return and let my actions reflect your love. Amen.

True kindness is found in the moments we give without counting the cost.

LETTING GO OF ENVY

A heart at peace gives life to the body, but envy rots the bones.
Proverbs 14:30

DEVOTIONAL

Letting go of envy is about lifting others up; true joy comes from celebrating their victories rather than resenting them.

What do you wish you had that someone else possesses, and how often do those thoughts affect how you view yourself and your relationships?

PRAYER

God, help me see my worth through your eyes. Teach me to celebrate others and let go of envy so I can find joy in my own journey. Amen.

True greatness isn't defined by what you have; it's found in the strength to appreciate what you've been given.

MAY 5

DEALING WITH INJUSTICE

When justice is done, it brings joy to the righteous but terror to evildoers.
Proverbs 21:15

DEVOTIONAL

Injustice can feel overwhelming, but remember that your response defines
your character, not the actions of others.

*What have you experienced that feels unfair, and how can you respond in a
way that reflects your values and beliefs?*

PRAYER

God, help me to see beyond the injustices I face. Give me strength to
respond with grace and wisdom, even when it feels tough. Amen.

Injustice can become your teacher; let it guide you toward
the strength of your character.

MAY 6

GOD CARES ABOUT MY STRUGGLES

*"Come to me, all you who are weary and burdened, and I will give you rest.
Take my yoke upon you and learn from me, for I am gentle and humble in
heart, and you will find rest for your souls. For my yoke is easy and my
burden is light."* **Matthew 11:28-30**

You're not alone in your struggles; God is there, ready to help you
carry your burdens.

DEVOTIONAL

*What struggles have you faced lately that make you feel isolated or
overwhelmed? How might remembering that God cares about you change
the way you approach these challenges?*

PRAYER

Dear God, thank you for being a constant support in my life. Help me to see
your presence during my struggles and remind me that I am never alone.

Even in your toughest moments, God's love is a light guiding you through.

GIVING GOD MY DREAMS

And my God will meet all your needs according to the riches of his glory in Christ Jesus. **Philippians 4:19**

DEVOTIONAL

Sometimes, the dreams we hold tightly to aren't the plans God has for us, but He has something even better in store.

What dreams do you hold in your heart that you haven't yet shared with God? How would it feel to let Him in on those secret hopes and plans?

PRAYER

God, I come before you today with my dreams—both big and small. Help me to trust in your plan for my life and give me the courage to hand over my ambitions to you. May I find peace in knowing that you are guiding my path.

When we give God our dreams, we invite His purpose and direction into our lives.

WHAT TO DO WHEN I'M CONFUSED

But when he, the Spirit of truth, comes, he will guide you into all the truth. He will not speak on his own; he will speak only what he hears, and he will tell you what is yet to come. **John 16:13**

DEVOTIONAL

You don't have to have all the answers today; trust that it's okay to explore and seek guidance as you navigate your choices.

What are some things in your life right now that are leaving you feeling confused or uncertain? How can you take a moment to pause and reflect on what truly matters to you?

PRAYER

Dear God, grant me clarity in my confusion and help me find peace in your presence. Guide me as I seek answers and remind me that it's okay to take my time.

In confusion, we often discover the shape of our own questions.

LOVING PEOPLE I DISAGREE WITH

For the entire law is fulfilled in keeping this one command: "Love your neighbor as yourself." **Galatians 5:14**

DEVOTIONAL

When faced with disagreements, remember that loving someone doesn't mean you have to agree with them; it means genuinely understanding and respecting them.

What would it look like for you to love someone you disagree with? How can you show kindness or understanding toward them, even when your views clash?

PRAYER

God, help me to see beyond my disagreements and to love others for who they are. Fill my heart with compassion and understanding for those around me, just as You love each of us without conditions.

True love is found in embracing our differences.

THE POWER OF FORGIVENESS

Bear with each other and forgive one another if any of you has a grievance against someone. Forgive as the Lord forgave you. **Colossians 3:13**

DEVOTIONAL

Forgiveness isn't just about letting someone off the hook; it's about freeing yourself to live a better life.

What does forgiveness mean to you in your life right now? Can you think of someone you need to forgive or ask for forgiveness? How might that change your relationship with them and how you feel inside?

PRAYER

Dear God, help me to understand the power of forgiveness. Fill my heart with the strength to let go of grudges and offer grace to others, just as You have given me grace. Thank You for always being there for me.

Forgiveness is not just a gift to others; it's a release for your own heart.

BEING GRATEFUL EVERY DAY

Give thanks to the Lord, for he is good; his love endures forever. **Psalm 107:1**

DEVOTIONAL

Imagine if every time something good happened—like scoring that game-winning goal or acing a tough exam—you took a moment to appreciate where that blessing came from. A simple thank you to God can really change your outlook. Every day holds a chance to find something to be thankful for, and that attitude can completely transform how you see your life.

What are three things you're grateful for today, and how can focusing on them change your perspective for the rest of your day?

PRAYER

Dear God, thank you for the many blessings in my life. Help me to see and appreciate all that you provide each day. May I carry an attitude of gratitude in everything I do.

Gratitude turns what we have into enough.

WHAT MAKES A REAL MAN

But the fruit of the Spirit is love, joy, peace, forbearance, kindness, goodness, faithfulness, gentleness and self-control. Against such things there is no law. **Galatians 5:22-23**

DEVOTIONAL

A real man stands out by embracing vulnerability and showing genuine kindness to others. This is the game plan for being a man: showing who you really are by how you treat others, not by how tough you act.

What does being a real man mean to you, and how do you see those qualities in the people around you?

PRAYER

Lord, help me understand the true meaning of manhood and guide me to embody the strength and kindness that define a real man. Teach me to stand firm in my values and be a light to others.

Real men are those who lead with their hearts and serve with their hands.

REJECTING LABELS

Since you are precious and honored in my sight, and because I love you, I will give people in exchange for you, nations in exchange for your life.
Isaiah 43:4

DEVOTIONAL
Don't let others define who you are; you are a unique blend of interests, talents, and passions.

What labels have you felt pressured to wear, and how have they shaped your view of yourself?

PRAYER
Dear God, help me see beyond the labels that others place on me. Fill my heart with the truth of who I am in You. Amen.

You are more than what others say; you are uniquely made for a purpose.

GOD CAN USE MY PAIN

Now I want you to know, brothers and sisters, that what has happened to me has actually served to advance the gospel. **Philippians 1:12**

DEVOTIONAL
Your pain doesn't have to define you; it can refine you and help others along the way.

What pain or struggle are you facing right now that you feel could never lead to something good? Have you considered how God might use it in your life or in the lives of others?

PRAYER
Dear God, thank you for being with us in our pain. Help us to see that, even in our toughest moments, you can bring about change and purpose. Amen.

Pain can be a pathway to purpose.

WHEN I FEEL SPIRITUALLY DRY

Therefore, since we are surrounded by such a great cloud of witnesses, let us throw off everything that hinders and the sin that so easily entangles. And let us run with perseverance the race marked out for us, fixing our eyes on Jesus, the pioneer and perfecter of faith. For the joy set before him he endured the cross, scorning its shame, and sat down at the right hand of the throne of God. **Hebrews 12:1-2**

DEVOTIONAL

When you're feeling spiritually dry, don't hesitate to reach out to God; He's there to help you regain your strength and purpose.

What do you think is causing you to feel spiritually dry right now? Are there things in your life that distract you from your connection with God, or do you simply need a moment to recharge?

PRAYER

God, I come to you today feeling a bit empty and in need of your love and guidance. Help me to draw closer to you in this dry season, and remind me that you're always there, even when I feel distant.

Even the strongest streams can run dry, but with patience and faith, the rains will come again.

CARING FOR THE LEAST POPULAR

"The King will reply, 'Truly I tell you, whatever you did for one of the least of these brothers and sisters of mine, you did for me.'" **Matthew 25:40**

DEVOTIONAL

Every small act of kindness can make a big difference in someone's life.

What does it look like for you to reach out to someone in your school or community who might feel left out or unnoticed? Have you ever noticed someone sitting alone or feeling down? How can you step in and make a difference in their day?

PRAYER

Dear God, help me see those around me who might be feeling lonely or forgotten. Give me the courage to reach out and show them they matter. Amen.

Caring for the least popular can be the greatest act of love.

MAY 17

AVOIDING GOSSIP

Those who consider themselves religious and yet do not keep a tight rein on their tongues deceive themselves, and their religion is worthless. **James 1:26**

DEVOTIONAL

If we think we're religious but can't control our tongues, we're fooling ourselves. It's like trying to play a video game with broken controls—no matter how good you are, it just doesn't work. Before you speak, consider whether your words could hurt someone. Choose to build others up instead of tearing them down.

What conversations have you overheard or participated in that felt more like gossip than genuine concern? How did those words affect you and others involved?

PRAYER

Dear God, help me to guard my words and fill my heart with kindness. Teach me to uplift others instead of tearing them down, and give me the wisdom to walk away from gossip.

Your words have the power to build someone up or tear them down—choose wisely.

MAY 18

WHY CHURCH MATTERS

"For where two or three gather in my name, there am I with them." **Matthew 18:20**

DEVOTIONAL

Being part of a church community helps you grow spiritually, connect with others, and find joy in shared experiences.

What do you think you gain from being part of a church community, and how does it shape your understanding of faith?

PRAYER

God, thank you for the gift of community and the opportunity to grow together in faith. Help me to see the value in gathering with others and deepen my connection to You through the church. Amen.

Church isn't just a place; it's a family that grows together in faith and support.

WHY BAPTISM MATTERS

"Therefore go and make disciples of all nations, baptizing them in the name of the Father and of the Son and of the Holy Spirit, and teaching them to obey everything I have commanded you. And surely I am with you always, to the very end of the age." **Matthew 28:19-20**

DEVOTIONAL

When you get baptized, you're telling the world you're serious about following Christ, and that matters more than you might think. Take this: Baptism is your moment to publicly say "I'm all in" for your faith, marking a fresh start in your personal journey with God.

What does baptism mean to you personally, and how does it connect with your journey of faith and identity? Take a moment to think about how this act might symbolize your own commitment and relationship with God.

PRAYER

Dear God, thank You for the gift of baptism and the way it symbolizes our new life in You. Help me understand its significance and embrace my identity as part of Your family.

Baptism is not just a symbol; it's a powerful step in your faith journey that connects you deeper to God and His purpose for your life.

LIVING THE GOSPEL, NOT JUST PREACHING IT

To do what is right and just is more acceptable to the Lord than sacrifice.
Proverbs 21:3

DEVOTIONAL

Don't just talk about being a good person; be the example that others can look up to.

What does it look like for you to live the Gospel every day? In your school, with your friends, and at home, how can your actions reflect your faith more than your words?

PRAYER

Dear God, help me to embody Your love and truth in all I do. Teach me to be a living example of the Gospel, so that my life can inspire others to know You.

Your actions often speak louder than your words; let them echo the truth of the Gospel.

MAY 21

AVOIDING DOUBLE LIFE

So whether you eat or drink or whatever you do, do it all for the glory of God.
1 Corinthians 10:31

DEVOTIONAL
Living authentically brings freedom, while a double life only leads to exhaustion and confusion.

What areas of your life feel like they don't match up? Are there parts of yourself you hide from family and friends? Take a moment to think about how living a double life can affect you and those around you. How can you become a more authentic version of yourself today?

PRAYER
Dear God, help me to be true to myself and to You. Give me strength to align my actions with my beliefs and to live without fear of judgment. Thank You for always loving me, even when I struggle.

Authenticity shines brighter than any mask we wear.

MAY 22

BEING A LIGHT ONLINE

For you were once darkness, but now you are light in the Lord. Live as children of light (for the fruit of the light consists in all goodness, righteousness and truth). **Ephesians 5:8-9**

DEVOTIONAL
Every time you engage online, remember you have the power to influence the mood and direction of conversations, so choose to shine brightly.

What does it mean for you to shine your light when you're scrolling through social media? How can your online presence reflect the values you hold dear in real life?

PRAYER
Dear God, help me to be a light in the digital world. Guide my thoughts and actions online, so I can reflect Your love and kindness to everyone I meet.

Your words and actions can be a beacon of hope in someone else's darkness.

NOT JUST A SUNDAY CHRISTIAN

"Why do you call me, 'Lord, Lord,' and do not do what I say?" **Luke 6:46**

DEVOTIONAL

Being a Christian isn't just about showing up on Sundays; it's about living out your faith every single day.

What does it mean to you to live out your faith every day, not just when you're at church? How do you express your beliefs in school, with friends, and at home?

PRAYER

God, help me to live authentically for You, seeking Your guidance in every part of my life. May my actions reflect my faith, shining Your light in the world around me.

Faith isn't just a Sunday activity; it's a daily adventure.

BEING CONSISTENT WITH MY WORDS

All you need to say is simply 'Yes' or 'No'; anything beyond this comes from the evil one. **Matthew 5:37**

DEVOTIONAL

In simple terms, mean what you say and say what you mean. It's about being true to your word. Being consistent with your words builds trust and shows others that you can be counted on.

What do your words say about who you are? How do you want others to see you based on what you say every day?

PRAYER

God, help me to use my words wisely and consistently. Let each word I speak reflect your truth and love in my life. Teach me to be a person of integrity whose words build others up.

Your words have the power to shape your world and the hearts of those around you.

FINDING GOD IN NATURE

And they were calling to one another: "Holy, holy, holy is the Lord Almighty; the whole earth is full of his glory. **Isaiah 6:3**

DEVOTIONAL
Nature is one of the best ways for you to experience God's presence; all you have to do is take a moment to look around and appreciate the beauty. When you're in nature, remember that it's not just scenery; it's a vivid reminder that there's a Creator who loves you.

What are some ways you've seen God's presence in the world around you? How does being in nature make you feel closer to Him?

PRAYER
God, thank you for the beauty of your creation. Help me to see your hand in the world around me and to find peace in your presence. Amen.

Nature is God's way of reminding us that beauty and strength exist in every detail of life.

CHOOSING PEACE OVER DRAMA

Peacemakers who sow in peace reap a harvest of righteousness. **James 3:18**

DEVOTIONAL
When faced with conflict or drama, remember that you have the power to choose peace, and that choice can change the atmosphere around you.

What situations in your life tend to pull you into unnecessary drama? How can you actively choose peace in those moments instead?

PRAYER
God, help me recognize the moments when drama tries to take over my life. Grant me the strength and wisdom to choose peace, so I can reflect Your love to those around me. Amen.

Drama fades, but peace remains.

WHEN GOD SAYS WAIT

But those who hope in the Lord will renew their strength. They will soar on wings like eagles; they will run and not grow weary, they will walk and not be faint. **Isaiah 40:31**

DEVOTIONAL

Waiting can be frustrating, but it often leads to growth and prepares you for the next big opportunity God has in store.

What are some areas in your life where you feel like God is asking you to wait? How can you trust Him in that waiting period?

PRAYER

Dear God, thank you for always being there, even when we find ourselves waiting. Help me to embrace the pause and remember that Your timing is perfect.

Patience is not just waiting; it's how we keep our hearts ready during the wait.

FOCUSING ON GOD'S VOICE

The Lord came and stood there, calling as at the other times, "Samuel! Samuel!" Then Samuel said, "Speak, for your servant is listening."
1 Samuel 3:10

DEVOTIONAL

The most important guidance you'll receive in life comes from tuning into God's voice, even when everything around you feels chaotic.

What distractions in your life might be drowning out God's voice? How can you create space to hear Him more clearly?

PRAYER

God, help me tune in to Your voice amidst the noise of life. Teach me to pause, listen, and follow where You lead me today.

Hearing God's voice requires silence; often, it's in the quiet moments that we discover the loudest truths.

TRUSTING GOD WITH MY TALENTS

We have different gifts, according to the grace given to each of us. If your gift is prophesying, then prophesy in accordance with your faith. **Romans 12:6**

DEVOTIONAL

Trust that your talents are part of a bigger plan, and have the courage to share them with the world. This means every talent you have is special and comes from God, so don't underestimate yourself. Even if you're not the star athlete or the top student, your unique abilities matter.

What are the unique talents you have, and how can you begin to trust God in using them for a greater purpose in your life?

PRAYER

God, help me to see the talents you've given me and to have the courage to trust you as I develop and share them. Guide my steps and let my abilities shine for your glory.

Your gifts are not just for you; they are meant to light up the world around you.

BEING KNOWN BY MY LOVE

"I am the good shepherd; I know my sheep and my sheep know me—" **John 10:14**

DEVOTIONAL

The most important thing is that God knows you completely and loves you fiercely, and that's what really matters.

What does it mean for you to be truly known by someone, and how can you reflect that love in your own friendships and relationships? Consider the ways you show love to others and how that reveals your true self.

PRAYER

God, thank You for knowing me completely and loving me unconditionally. Help me to embrace that love and share it with those around me. May my friendships be rooted in genuine connection and honest affection.

Being known is the beginning of loving and being loved in return.

STANDING FIRM IN TEMPTATION

No temptation has overtaken you except what is common to mankind. And God is faithful; he will not let you be tempted beyond what you can bear. But when you are tempted, he will also provide a way out so that you can endure it. **1 Corinthians 10:13**

DEVOTIONAL
When you face temptation, remember that staying true to yourself takes courage, and the right friends will respect your decisions.

What are some specific temptations you faced this week, and how can you lean on your faith to stand firm against them? Think about moments when it was tough to make the right choice.

PRAYER
Dear God, thank You for always being there to help us through tough times. Please give me the strength to resist temptation and choose what's right, even when it's hard.

Strength grows in moments when you choose principle over pleasure.

JUNE 1

LETTING GOD SHAPE MY IDENTITY

For you died, and your life is now hidden with Christ in God. **Colossians 3:3**

DEVOTIONAL
Your identity is not defined by what others think or say about you
but by who God says you are.

What does it mean for you to let God define who you are rather than the world around you? Can you think of a time when you felt pressure to fit in that made you question your true self?

PRAYER
God, thank You for creating me uniquely and loving me just as I am. Help me to rely on Your truth to shape my identity and guide me through my struggles. I trust in Your plan for my life.

Your true identity is found in the one who made you, not in the opinions of others.

JUNE 2

HOW TO SAY SORRY

Make every effort to live in peace with everyone and to be holy; without holiness no one will see the Lord. **Hebrews 12:14**

DEVOTIONAL
Sometimes, saying sorry is the bravest thing you can do, and it can mend what was broken if you're willing to own up to your mistakes.

What does saying sorry mean to you? Can you recall a time when you found it hard to apologize? How did it make you feel, and how do you think the other person felt?

PRAYER
Dear God, help me to find the courage to say sorry when I've hurt someone. Teach me the value of humility and the strength it takes to make things right. I want to be a person who builds bridges rather than walls.

Saying sorry is not a sign of weakness; it's the first step towards healing and growth.

JUNE 3

OVERCOMING LAZINESS

Diligent hands will rule, but laziness ends in forced labor. **Proverbs 12:24**

DEVOTIONAL

Don't let laziness steal your time; be the one who takes charge and makes things happen.

What are some small habits you can start today to overcome laziness and achieve your goals? Think about how you can tackle one task at a time and feel the satisfaction of progress.

PRAYER

Dear God, help me find the motivation and strength to rise above laziness. Guide my thoughts and actions today, and let me embrace the opportunities for growth that you place in my path.

Great things are achieved not by the grand gestures,
but by the small steps we take every day.

JUNE 4

TAKING CARE OF MY BODY

Do you not know that your bodies are temples of the Holy Spirit, who is in you, whom you have received from God? You are not your own; you were bought at a price. Therefore honor God with your bodies.
1 Corinthians 6:19-20

DEVOTIONAL

Taking care of your body is not just about looking good; it's about feeling good and being ready for whatever comes your way.

What are some small changes you can make today to show your body the care it deserves? Think about how what you eat, how you move, and even how you rest can change the way you feel each day.

PRAYER

Dear God, thank you for the incredible body you've given me. Help me to honor it through healthy choices and to see it as a temple of your Spirit. Amen.

Your body is not just a vessel; it's the instrument through which you experience life.

JUNE 5

LIVING FOR AN AUDIENCE OF ONE

Fear of man will prove to be a snare, but whoever trusts in the Lord is kept safe. *Proverbs 29:25*

DEVOTIONAL
Live your life for God, not for the approval of those around you.

What does it really mean for you to live your life as if God is the only audience that matters? Are there areas in your life where you feel pressure to impress others instead of staying true to yourself and your beliefs?

PRAYER
Dear God, help me focus on living for You above all else. Remind me that Your love and approval are what truly matters. Teach me to find joy in being authentic and true to who You've made me to be.

To live for an audience of One is to find freedom in your true identity.

JUNE 6

SPENDING MONEY WISELY

For the love of money is a root of all kinds of evil. Some people, eager for money, have wandered from the faith and pierced themselves with many griefs. *1 Timothy 6:10*

DEVOTIONAL
Spend your money in ways that build up your life and relationships, not just for short-lived thrills.

What does spending money wisely mean to you? How can you make choices today that reflect your values and future goals? Take a moment to think about how each decision affects not just today, but your tomorrow as well.

PRAYER
Dear God, help me to see the value of my money and guide me in making choices that honor you and my future. Teach me the difference between wants and needs, so I can spend wisely. Amen.

True wealth is not what you have, but how you manage what you possess.

JUNE 7

USING MY FREE TIME FOR GOOD

Those who work their land will have abundant food, but those who chase fantasies have no sense. **Proverbs 12:11**

DEVOTIONAL

Don't let your free time slip away — use it to make a positive impact on yourself and those around you.

What do you think you could accomplish with an hour of your free time if you dedicated it to something good, positive, or meaningful?

PRAYER

Dear God, thank you for the gift of time and the opportunities it brings. Help me to use my free time wisely, choosing actions that reflect Your love and purpose.

Every minute can be a chance to make a difference.

JUNE 8

LOVING GOD MORE THAN COMFORT

Do not love the world or anything in the world. If anyone loves the world, love for the Father is not in them. For everything in the world—the lust of the flesh, the lust of the eyes, and the pride of life—comes not from the Father but from the world. 17 The world and its desires pass away, but whoever does the will of God lives forever. **1 John 2:15-17**

DEVOTIONAL

Remember that chasing after comfort and fitting in might feel good in the moment, but it won't last. Real love for God means prioritizing Him over everything else that pulls at our hearts. Life isn't about always seeking comfort; it's about following God, even when the road gets tough.

What would it look like for you to step out of your comfort zone to show your love for God? Are there areas in your life where you feel God is calling you to take a risk for Him?

PRAYER

Dear God, help me to love You more than my comfort. Teach me to trust in You, even when it feels challenging. I want to embrace the risks that come from following You wholeheartedly.

Love for God isn't measured by the ease of our journey but by the courage of our steps.

JUNE 9

BEING A MAN OF MY WORD

Above all, my brothers and sisters, do not swear—not by heaven or by earth or by anything else. All you need to say is a simple "Yes" or "No." Otherwise you will be condemned. **James 5:12**

DEVOTIONAL
Always be true to your word; it builds respect and deepens friendships.

What does it mean to you to keep your promises, both to yourself and to others? Can you think of a time when being a man of your word really mattered in your life?

PRAYER
God, help me to be someone who keeps my promises and honors my word. Teach me the strength and integrity it takes to be reliable in all that I say and do. Amen.

Character is not just what you say; it's what you do when no one is watching.

JUNE 10

DOING HARD THINGS

All hard work brings a profit, but mere talk leads only to poverty.
Proverbs 14:23

DEVOTIONAL
The effort you put into overcoming tough challenges can lead to extraordinary growth and achievement.

What hard thing have you been avoiding that you know you need to face? How would conquering that challenge change you for the better?

PRAYER
Dear God, give me the courage to face the hard things in my life. Help me to see challenges as opportunities for growth and strength. Amen.

Strength isn't just about muscles; it's about the bravery to tackle what seems impossible.

TURNING TO GOD IN PAIN

I consider that our present sufferings are not worth comparing with the glory that will be revealed in us. **Romans 8:18**

DEVOTIONAL
Even in our toughest times, turning to God can reveal new strengths we never knew we had.

What does it feel like for you when you're facing tough times? Do you ever remember to reach out to God in those moments?

PRAYER
God, in my pain, help me to see your love surrounding me. Teach me to lean on you and trust that brighter days are ahead. I know you're with me always.

Even in our darkest moments, God's light can guide us back to hope.

FAITH THAT LASTS

Consequently, faith comes from hearing the message, and the message is heard through the word about Christ. **Romans 10:17**

DEVOTIONAL
True faith isn't just a one-time decision; it's a daily commitment that grows through the ups and downs of life.

What does it mean for you to have faith that endures during tough times? Can you think of a moment where your faith was tested, and how you responded?

PRAYER
Dear God, thank you for always being there for me, even when my faith feels shaky. Help me to trust in You and strengthen my belief so that it lasts all my life.

Faith isn't just something we say; it's the way we live every single day.

BEING HUMBLE IN SUCCESS

Humble yourselves before the Lord, and he will lift you up. **James 4:10**

DEVOTIONAL

This isn't just about lowering your head; it's about keeping your heart in check when you're on top of your game. When you score that winning goal or ace that exam, remember that your talents are gifts, not just your own doing. Always remember that true strength lies in lifting others up, not just yourself.

What does success look like for you, and how can you stay grounded while achieving your goals? Think about ways you've been recognized for your talents and how you can use those gifts to uplift others.

PRAYER

Dear God, thank You for the successes and talents You have given me. Help me to remember to stay humble and use my strengths to serve others and not just myself. Guide me to be a light for those around me.

Success is not about how high you climb, but how deeply you can stay rooted.

CHOOSING PEACE IN CONFLICT

Make every effort to keep the unity of the Spirit through the bond of peace. **Ephesians 4:3**

DEVOTIONAL

When faced with conflict, how you respond can either escalate the situation or bring about harmony, so think before you act.

What situations in your life stir up conflict or tension? How might choosing peace in those moments change the outcome for you and those around you?

PRAYER

God, help me find calm in the chaos. Grant me the strength to seek peace and wisdom in my responses, especially when things heat up. Amen.

Peace isn't the absence of conflict, but the presence of a calm heart.

HOW TO HAVE A REAL TALK WITH GOD

Let us then approach God's throne of grace with confidence, so that we may receive mercy and find grace to help us in our time of need.
Hebrews 4:16

DEVOTIONAL

Think about that—God wants us to come to Him boldly, like a friend, sharing our struggles and dreams without fear. It's a reminder that prayer isn't just for the serious moments; it's for every part of our lives. Having real talk with God can transform your worries into peace and your fears into strength.

What does your current conversation with God sound like? Is it honest and open, or more like a list of requests? Take a moment to think about how you can deepen that dialogue and make it more personal.

PRAYER

Dear God, thank You for always being there, listening to my heart. Help me to speak honestly with You today, sharing my thoughts and feelings without holding back. Amen.

Real talk with God is about opening up your heart and letting Him in.

WHEN I'M TIRED OF TRYING

I can do all this through him who gives me strength. **Philippians 4:13**

DEVOTIONAL

Even when you feel exhausted and defeated, remember that true strength comes from leaning on God.

What are some areas in your life where you feel like you're giving everything but not seeing the results you want?

PRAYER

God, I'm feeling worn out and overwhelmed. Please renew my strength and help me remember that I'm never alone in my struggles. Guide me to find peace and encouragement in Your presence.

Sometimes the weight of the world feels heavy, but it's in those moments we can lean into God's strength.

GOD KNOWS WHAT I NEED

Nothing in all creation is hidden from God's sight. Everything is uncovered and laid bare before the eyes of him to whom we must give account.
Hebrews 4:13

DEVOTIONAL

God understands the pressures we face and knows exactly what we need—whether it's strength, guidance, or simply a break. Trust that God sees you in your struggles and provides what you truly need, even when it feels overwhelming.

What do you think you really need right now in your life, and have you taken a moment to share that with God?

PRAYER

Dear God, I thank You for knowing me better than I know myself. Please help me trust in Your plan, knowing that You understand what I need at this very moment.

God's provision often comes disguised as a quiet assurance in our hearts.

STANDING STRONG AFTER FAILURE

But when he saw the wind, he was afraid and, beginning to sink, cried out, "Lord, save me!" Immediately Jesus reached out his hand and caught him. "You of little faith," he said, "why did you doubt?" **Matthew 14:30-31**

DEVOTIONAL

When you face failure, remember it's just one moment in your journey; what matters is how you choose to rise and grow from it.

What's one failure you've experienced recently, and how can you see it as a stepping stone for your growth rather than a dead end?

PRAYER

Dear God, thank you for always being there, even when we stumble. Help me to see my failures as opportunities to learn and grow stronger. Amen.

Every setback is just a setup for a comeback.

JUNE 19

BELIEVING GOD'S PROMISES

Yet he did not waver through unbelief regarding the promise of God, but was strengthened in his faith and gave glory to God, being fully persuaded that God had power to do what he had promised. **Romans 4:20-21**

DEVOTIONAL

When you trust in God's promises and give your best effort, you might just see yourself rise to your potential in ways you never expected.

What promises has God made in your life that you need to hold onto today? Can you think of a time when trusting Him made a difference for you?

PRAYER

Dear God, thank You for always being faithful to Your promises. Help me to trust You more and lean on Your words when I feel uncertain or overwhelmed. Teach me to see Your hand in my life every day.

God's promises are like a strong anchor for your soul, steadying you through life's storms.

JUNE 20

COURAGE TO BE MYSELF

Be strong and courageous. Do not be afraid or terrified because of them, for the Lord your God goes with you; he will never leave you nor forsake you."
Deuteronomy 31:6

DEVOTIONAL

True courage is being yourself, even when it feels tough; your authenticity can encourage others to do the same.

What does it mean for you to be yourself, and how can you show that courage in your daily life?

PRAYER

Dear God, help me to find strength in being who You've created me to be. Give me the courage to embrace my unique qualities and to share them confidently with the world around me.

Courage is not the absence of fear, but the triumph over it.

JUNE 21

WHAT IF I MESS UP AGAIN?

If we confess our sins, he is faithful and just and will forgive us our sins and purify us from all unrighteousness. **1 John 1:9**

DEVOTIONAL

Messing up is part of life, but it's how you respond to those mistakes that truly defines you.

What fears or doubts come to mind when you think about messing up again? How can you remind yourself of the strength you have in moving forward?

PRAYER

Hey God, I'm feeling a bit overwhelmed by the thought of messing up again. Help me to know that it's okay to be imperfect and give me the courage to keep trying, no matter how many times I fall.

Failure is not the end; it's a stepping stone towards growth.

JUNE 22

LIVING OUT MY FAITH AT HOME

Love must be sincere. Hate what is evil; cling to what is good. Be devoted to one another in love. Honor one another above yourselves. **Romans 12:9-10**

DEVOTIONAL

When you're living out your faith at home, even the small actions of standing up for those you love can make a big impact.

What does it mean for you to show your faith in your everyday life at home, especially in how you treat your family and manage your responsibilities?

PRAYER

God, help me to live out my faith authentically at home. Teach me to love my family, respect my space, and reflect Your light in my actions. Amen.

Your faith shines brightest in the familiarity of home.

LISTENING MORE, TALKING LESS

To answer before listening— that is folly and shame. **Proverbs 18:13**

DEVOTIONAL

Listening more and talking less can make a huge difference in how we connect with those around us.

What would it look like for you to listen more and talk less this week? Can you think of a situation where choosing to listen could make a difference in your relationships or understanding?

PRAYER

Dear God, help me to find the strength and patience to listen more than I speak. Teach me the art of understanding others and guide my heart to reflect Your love in my interactions.

Listening is a gift that opens the door to understanding.

TRUSTING GOD IN FRIENDSHIP

Every good and perfect gift is from above, coming down from the Father of the heavenly lights, who does not change like shifting shadows. **James 1:17**

DEVOTIONAL

When things get tough in friendships, remember to lean on God, who gives you the strength to be a friend that others can trust.

What does it look like for you to trust God in your friendships? Are there times you feel uncertain about who to rely on or how to navigate complications with your friends?

PRAYER

Dear God, thank You for the friends You've placed in my life. Help me to lean on You as I navigate these relationships and to trust that You are guiding me in every interaction.

True friendship is a gift that reflects His love and strengthens our faith.

THE POWER OF SMALL ACTS

In the same way, faith by itself, if it is not accompanied by action, is dead.
James 2:17

DEVOTIONAL
You may never know how much a little kindness can mean to someone else, so be brave enough to reach out and be a friend when you see someone in need.

What is one small act of kindness you can do this week that could lighten someone else's load?

PRAYER
Dear God, help me to see the opportunities for kindness around me. Let my actions reflect Your love and make a difference in the lives of others.

Even the smallest gesture can create ripples of change.

MY LIFE CAN INSPIRE OTHERS

The fool says in his heart, "There is no God." They are corrupt, their deeds are vile; there is no one who does good. **Psalm 14:1**

DEVOTIONAL
You have the power to uplift those around you, and by doing so, you create a ripple effect of inspiration that can touch lives beyond your own.

What are some ways you've seen your actions or words inspire someone else? Can you think of a moment when you made a difference, even in a small way?

PRAYER
Dear God, thank you for the unique gifts you've given me. Help me to recognize the ways I can inspire others and guide me in using my life to shine your light.

Your story can be the spark that ignites someone else's journey.

JUNE 27

LETTING GO OF CONTROL

Now listen, you who say, "Today or tomorrow we will go to this or that city, spend a year there, carry on business and make money." Why, you do not even know what will happen tomorrow. What is your life? You are a mist that appears for a little while and then vanishes. Instead, you ought to say, "If it is the Lord's will, we will live and do this or that." **James 4:13-15**

DEVOTIONAL

Let go of the need to control everything in life; sometimes surrender opens the door to greater experiences and unexpected blessings.

What are the areas in your life where you feel the need to control everything? How does that impact your relationships and your own peace of mind?

PRAYER

Dear God, help me to recognize the things I can't control and to trust You with them. Grant me the peace to let go of my worries and embrace Your guidance in my life. Amen.

Letting go doesn't mean giving up; it means trusting God to take the wheel.

JUNE 28

GIVING GOD MY PAST

Therefore, there is now no condemnation for those who are in Christ Jesus. **Romans 8:1**

DEVOTIONAL

When you surrender your past to God, you gain the freedom to become the person you're meant to be.

What parts of your past are you still holding onto that you need to let go of? Can you think of moments or choices that have shaped you but no longer define you?

PRAYER

Dear God, I come before You with my past—my mistakes, regrets, and experiences. Help me to release these burdens into Your hands and find freedom in Your forgiveness. Amen.

Your history doesn't have to be your destiny.

JUNE 29
LEARNING TO LEAD NOW

"Not so with you. Instead, whoever wants to become great among you must be your servant, and whoever wants to be first must be your slave— just as the Son of Man did not come to be served, but to serve, and to give his life as a ransom for many." **Matthew 20:26-28**

DEVOTIONAL

The greatest leaders are often those who serve others, showing that you don't have to wait until you're older to make a real impact.

What does leadership look like in your everyday life? How can you start to step up and lead, even in small ways, with your friends, family, or in school? Consider how your actions can inspire others around you.

PRAYER

Dear God, help me to recognize the opportunities to lead in my life. Give me the courage to take those steps and the wisdom to guide others with kindness and integrity. Amen.

Leadership isn't about being the boss; it's about being a positive influence.

JUNE 30
HOW TO SPOT REAL FRIENDS

And let us consider how we may spur one another on toward love and good deeds, not giving up meeting together, as some are in the habit of doing, but encouraging one another—and all the more as you see the Day approaching. **Hebrews 10:24-25**

DEVOTIONAL

This verse reminds us that real friends are those who push us to grow and get better, not just hang out with us for fun. Real friends are the ones who respect you, who bring out the best in you, and who stand by you even when it's tough.

What qualities do you look for in a friend? Are they the ones who truly support you, even when times get tough? Take a moment to think about how you feel when you're around your different friends.

PRAYER

God, please help me to recognize and cherish the friends who lift me up and are loyal in all circumstances. Grant me wisdom to know the difference between a true friend and someone who just wants to be around for the good times. Thank you for the gift of friendship and the joy it brings into my life!

Real friends are like stars; you don't always see them, but you know they're always there.

JULY 1

MY VALUE ISN'T IN MY LOOKS

"Before I formed you in the womb I knew you, before you were born I set you apart; I appointed you as a prophet to the nations." **Jeremiah 1:5**

DEVOTIONAL

This verse reminds you that your worth is rooted deep in who you are, not what you look like on the outside. Your true worth is found in your character and talents, not your outer appearance.

What do you think makes you truly valuable? Is it your looks, your skills, or something deeper that defines who you are?

PRAYER

God, thank You for creating me in Your perfect image. Help me to see my worth beyond just appearances, and remind me that I am loved for who I am inside.

True value comes from the heart, not the mirror.

JULY 2

FINDING GOD IN MUSIC

He says, "I will declare your name to my brothers and sisters; in the assembly I will sing your praises." **Hebrews 2:12**

DEVOTIONAL

No matter where you are or what you're going through, remember that God can show up in the songs you love, bringing comfort, hope, and understanding.

What is a song that never fails to lift your spirits or connect you to something deeper? How does it make you feel, and what do you think God might be communicating through the music you love?

PRAYER

Dear God, thank you for the gift of music that speaks to our hearts. Help us to hear Your voice in the melodies and rhythms we encounter each day. May we find Your presence in every note!

Music has a way of expressing what our hearts often can't put into words.

JULY 3

FIGHTING TEMPTATION WITH SCRIPTURE

All Scripture is God-breathed and is useful for teaching, rebuking, correcting and training in righteousness, so that the servant of God may be thoroughly equipped for every good work. **2 Timothy 3:16-17**

DEVOTIONAL

When faced with temptation, remember that God's Word can help you stand strong and inspire others to choose better paths too.

What temptations do you face in your daily life, and how can Scripture help you resist them?

PRAYER

Dear God, help me to turn to Your Word when I'm tempted. Remind me of Your strength and love so that I can choose the right path. Amen.

Scripture is your sword; wield it wisely against temptation.

JULY 4

WHEN MY PRAYERS FEEL UNHEARD

Therefore confess your sins to each other and pray for each other so that you may be healed. The prayer of a righteous person is powerful and effective. **James 5:16**

DEVOTIONAL

When my prayers feel unheard, sometimes I need to step out and make the first move, because God might be inviting me to be a part of the solution.

What's one moment when you felt like your prayers weren't getting through? How did that make you feel, and what did you do next?

PRAYER

Dear God, even when it feels like you're distant, help me to trust that you hear my heart. Give me patience and strength to keep seeking you, even in silence. Thank you for being here with me.

Sometimes, silence in prayer isn't a sign of absence
but an invitation to deepen our trust.

REAL LOVE VS. FAKE LOVE

But God demonstrates his own love for us in this: While we were still sinners, Christ died for us. **Romans 5:8**

DEVOTIONAL

Real love is about being there for people, through the highs and lows, not just posting the best moments online.

What does love truly mean to you, and how can you tell the difference between real love that lifts you up and fake love that brings you down?

PRAYER

God, help me to recognize and embrace real love in my life. Guide my heart to discern genuine connections and give me the strength to distance myself from anything that feels false. Amen.

Real love challenges you to grow; fake love keeps you comfortable in your worst habits.

NOT LETTING ANGER WIN

Tremble and[g] do not sin; when you are on your beds, search your hearts and be silent. **Psalm 4:4**

DEVOTIONAL

When anger rises, take a step back, breathe, and choose to respond with grace rather than react in fury.

What situations in your life make you feel the most angry, and how can you take a step back to respond with kindness instead?

PRAYER

God, help me to recognize when anger starts to rise within me. Teach me to pause, breathe, and choose love over frustration. Fill my heart with peace and understanding, Amen.

Anger is a visitor; don't let it set up permanent residence in your heart.

LEARNING FROM CRITICISM

"Blessed is the one whom God corrects; so do not despise the discipline of the Almighty. For he wounds, but he also binds up; he injures, but his hands also heal. **Job 5:17-18**

DEVOTIONAL

Embracing criticism can unlock your potential and lead you toward improvement, even when it feels uncomfortable.

What's one piece of criticism you've received that made you feel frustrated at first, but later helped you grow? How can you look at it differently now?

PRAYER

Dear God, help me to see the value in the feedback I receive, even when it's hard to hear. Teach me to grow stronger and wiser through every piece of criticism. Amen.

Every piece of feedback is a stepping stone on the path to becoming who you are meant to be.

SERVING WITH JOY

You, my brothers and sisters, were called to be free. But do not use your freedom to indulge the flesh; rather, serve one another humbly in love. **Galatians 5:13**

DEVOTIONAL

Serving others can transform your heart and brighten your days, so find joy in lifting others up and watch how it lifts you too.

What's one way you can serve someone in your life this week that brings you joy instead of feeling like a chore? How will you make that happen?

PRAYER

God, help me find joy in the little ways I can serve others. Give me the strength and courage to be a light in someone's day this week. Amen.

Serving others can be one of the greatest sources of joy in our own lives.

JULY 9

FAITH THAT GROWS

Therefore, since we have been justified through faith, we have peace with God through our Lord Jesus Christ. **Romans 5:1**

DEVOTIONAL

Faith isn't about never falling but about getting back up and continuing to trust in God through every twist and turn life throws at you.

What does your faith look like right now, and how can you nurture it to grow stronger over time? Take a moment to think about the small steps you can take each day to deepen your connection with God. Are there specific areas in your life where you're seeking more strength or guidance?

PRAYER

Dear God, thank you for being a constant presence in my life. Help me to trust in you and strengthen my faith so I can grow closer to you each day. Amen.

Faith is like a seed; when planted and nurtured, it grows beyond what we can see.

JULY 10

LOVING EVEN WHEN IT'S HARD

And he has given us this command: Anyone who loves God must also love their brother and sister. **1 John 4:21**

DEVOTIONAL

Sometimes, loving others means looking beyond our feelings and choosing to understand where they're coming from.

What does it look like for you to love someone even when you're feeling hurt or frustrated? Can you think of a time when you found it difficult to love, and how might you approach that situation differently now?

PRAYER

Dear God, help me to see others through Your eyes. Teach me how to love even when it's tough, and give me the strength to act with kindness and compassion. Amen.

True strength is shown in how we love when it costs us something.

JULY 11

LIVING WITH ETERNAL PERSPECTIVE

What good is it for someone to gain the whole world, yet forfeit their soul?
Mark 8:36

DEVOTIONAL
This world has some pretty cool stuff, but it's not worth losing sight of what really matters. Success is fleeting, but investing in relationships and helping others leaves a lasting impact.

What do you think it truly means to live with an eternal perspective, and how can it change the way you view your daily challenges or dreams?

PRAYER
Dear God, help me to see beyond the present moment and remind me of the bigger picture you have for my life. Give me strength and wisdom to make choices that honor You and reflect your eternal love.

Eternal perspective gives weight to your decisions today,
shaping who you are becoming tomorrow.

JULY 12

BEING A BROTHER OTHERS LOOK UP TO

How good and pleasant it is when God's people live together in unity!
Psalm 133:1

DEVOTIONAL
Being a brother to others means stepping up in the small moments and being the friend that everyone needs.

What does it mean to be a brother that others look up to? How can your actions and words inspire those around you to be their best selves? Think about the qualities you admire in other brothers or friends—how can you embody those in your own life?

PRAYER
Dear God, help me to be a brother who lifts others up. Guide my words and actions so that I can reflect kindness and strength to those around me. Amen.

Being a brother isn't just about blood; it's about building bonds that inspire and uplift.

WORSHIP IS MORE THAN MUSIC

Let everything that has breath praise the Lord. Praise the Lord. **Psalm 150:6**

DEVOTIONAL
Worship is shown through how you live and express yourself,
not just through music.

What does worship mean to you beyond the songs you sing? How do you express that love and devotion to God in your everyday life? Consider moments when your actions reflect your heart for Him.

PRAYER
God, thank you for being present in my life. Help me to see that worship is in all I do, and guide me to honor You with my thoughts, words, and actions each day.

Worship is the language of your heart, spoken through your actions and choices.

BEING BRAVE IN MY FAITH

The wicked flee though no one pursues, but the righteous are as bold as a lion. **Proverbs 28:1**

DEVOTIONAL
Being brave in your faith means standing up for what's right, even if it means being different from your friends.

What does it mean for you to stand strong in your faith, especially when it feels like everyone around you is going in a different direction? How can you take a small step today that shows your courage to live out your beliefs?

PRAYER
Dear God, help me to be brave in my faith, even when it's tough. Give me the strength to stand up for what I believe and to share Your love with those around me. Amen.

Bravery isn't the absence of fear; it's standing firm in what you believe, even when it scares you.

WHEN GOD FEELS SILENT

He says, "Be still, and know that I am God; I will be exalted among the nations, I will be exalted in the earth." **Psalm 46:10**

DEVOTIONAL

When life feels like it's spinning out of control, sometimes all you need is to pause and recognize that God is still in charge. When it seems like God's not speaking to you, remember that His presence can be felt in the quiet moments too.

What do you do when you feel like God isn't listening or is far away? How do you remind yourself of His presence in those quiet moments?

PRAYER

Dear God, help me to trust You even when I can't hear You. Encourage my heart and remind me that You are always with me, guiding me through the silence.

Sometimes, God's silence isn't absence; it's an invitation to grow deeper in faith.

HOPING IN HARD TIMES

May the God of hope fill you with all joy and peace as you trust in him, so that you may overflow with hope by the power of the Holy Spirit. **Romans 15:13**

DEVOTIONAL

Sometimes, it's in our hardest moments that we discover what real hope looks like, and leaning on God can turn setbacks into comebacks. When things get rough, that's when hope really counts, and God is right there to give us strength.

What challenges are you facing right now that make it hard to see the light at the end of the tunnel? How can you find hope in those moments?

PRAYER

Dear God, thank you for always being with us, even when times are tough. Help us to see Your light and find strength in hope, no matter what we face.

Hope is the anchor for our souls, keeping us steady through the storms of life.

JULY 17

LIVING BOLDLY FOR CHRIST

For I am not ashamed of the gospel, because it is the power of God that brings salvation to everyone who believes: first to the Jew, then to the Gentile. **Romans 1:16**

DEVOTIONAL

Dare to take a stand for your beliefs, knowing that your boldness can inspire others to find their own faith.

What does it mean for you to live boldly for Christ in your daily life? Are there areas where you feel you can take a stand or express your faith more openly?

PRAYER

Dear God, help me to have the courage to be bold in my faith. Give me the strength to shine Your light in my words and actions every day.

Faith isn't just a belief; it's a lifestyle that speaks volumes.

JULY 18

THE FREEDOM OF FORGIVENESS

So if the Son sets you free, you will be free indeed. **John 8:36**

DEVOTIONAL

Forgiveness isn't about letting others off the hook; it's about freeing yourself from the weight of anger and resentment.

What does forgiveness mean to you, and have you ever thought about how holding onto grudges can weigh you down instead of setting you free?

PRAYER

Dear God, help us learn the power of forgiveness. Teach us to let go of our anger and embrace the freedom that comes from forgiving ourselves and others. Amen.

Forgiveness isn't just letting go; it's choosing to embrace a new beginning.

JULY 19

REPLACING LIES WITH TRUTH

"Listen to me, you who pursue righteousness and who seek the Lord: Look to the rock from which you were cut and to the quarry from which you were hewn." **Isaiah 51:1**

DEVOTIONAL

Replace the lies about your limitations with the truth of your potential, and watch how it changes everything.

What lies do you find yourself believing about who you are or what you can achieve? How might your life change if you replaced those lies with the truth of who you are made to be?

PRAYER

Dear God, help me to see myself through Your eyes. Remind me of the truth about my worth and potential, and give me the strength to stand firm against the lies that try to pull me down.

Truth is the anchor that keeps your soul from drifting.

JULY 20

TRUSTING GOD WITH MY FUTURE

Do not be anxious about anything, but in every situation, by prayer and petition, with thanksgiving, present your requests to God. And the peace of God, which transcends all understanding, will guard your hearts and your minds in Christ Jesus. **Philippians 4:6-7**

DEVOTIONAL

Trusting God with your future means letting go of the worry and embracing the journey, knowing He has a plan for you.

What are your biggest hopes and fears about the future, and how can trusting God change your perspective on them?

PRAYER

Dear God, help me to release my worries about what lies ahead and to place my trust in Your perfect plan for my life. I know You are with me every step of the way.

Trusting God means believing in His promises when the path ahead is unclear.

HOW TO STAY SPIRITUALLY STRONG

I have hidden your word in my heart that I might not sin against you.
Psalm 119:11

DEVOTIONAL
Stay disciplined in your faith like you would in practice; it's the hidden strength that helps you through tough times.

What are the things in your life right now that challenge your faith, and how can you address them head-on? Consider where you might draw strength.

PRAYER
God, thank You for being our rock. Help me stand firm in my faith, even when life gets tough. Guide me each day to make choices that reflect Your love.

Stay rooted in faith, and you will grow stronger with every challenge.

BEING A MAN OF INTEGRITY

So that your daily life may win the respect of outsiders and so that you will not be dependent on anybody. **1 Thessalonians 4:12**

DEVOTIONAL
Being a man of integrity means doing what's right, even when it's easier to take the shortcut.

What does it mean to you to stand firm in your values, even when others around you might not? Are there moments in your life where you've been tempted to compromise on what you know is right?

PRAYER
Dear God, help me to be a man of integrity. Guide my choices and give me the strength to stand up for what is right, even when it's tough. Thank you for your love and support on this journey.

Integrity is doing the right thing, even when no one is watching.

GIVING GOD MY WORRIES

Cast your cares on the Lord and he will sustain you; he will never let the righteous be shaken. **Psalm 55:22**

DEVOTIONAL

Don't be afraid to hand over your worries to God; He's ready to help you face each challenge with strength and calm.

What are some worries you're holding onto right now, and how can you imagine letting them go by trusting God?

PRAYER

God, I bring my worries to you today. Help me to trust in your plan and find peace as I release what burdens me. Thank you for always being there to listen.

Sometimes, the best thing you can do is let go and let God guide your path.

RESPONDING TO HATE WITH LOVE

But I tell you, love your enemies and pray for those who persecute you. **Matthew 5:44**

DEVOTIONAL

When faced with hate, responding with love can transform not just your situation, but also the hearts of others.

What does it look like for you to respond with love when someone treats you unkindly? Can you think of a recent situation where you felt hate or negativity directed towards you? How might a loving response change the outcome?

PRAYER

Dear God, help me to see beyond anger and hurt. Fill my heart with your love so I can respond to negativity with kindness and compassion. Teach me to be a light in the darkness.

Love is the greatest weapon against hate.

CHOOSING GROWTH EVERY DAY

Let the wise listen and add to their learning, and let the discerning get guidance— **Proverbs 1:5**

DEVOTIONAL

Choose to embrace every day as a chance to learn and grow, even when it's tough.

What are some small steps you can take today that will help you grow into the person you want to become?

PRAYER

Dear God, help me to embrace each day as a new opportunity for growth. Give me the courage to face my challenges and the wisdom to learn from them. Amen.

Every day is a chance to be better than yesterday.

LETTING MY LIFE BE AN EXAMPLE

You became imitators of us and of the Lord, for you welcomed the message in the midst of severe suffering with the joy given by the Holy Spirit. And so you became a model to all the believers in Macedonia and Achaia. **1 Thessalonians 1:6-7**

DEVOTIONAL

Your willingness to be honest about your struggles can inspire others to be brave in their own lives.

What does it mean for you to live in a way that inspires others around you? How can your actions today reflect the values you want to stand for?

PRAYER

Dear God, help me to shine with your light in everything I do. Lead me to be a positive example for my friends and family, showing them your love through my actions.

Your life is the most powerful message you can share with the world.

JULY 27

BEING A SAFE PLACE FOR OTHERS

Carry each other's burdens, and in this way you will fulfill the law of Christ.
Galatians 6:2

DEVOTIONAL

Being a safe place for others means being someone who listens and cares, making a difference without needing to fix everything.

What does it mean for you to be a safe place for your friends? How can you create an environment where they feel comfortable sharing their thoughts and struggles with you?

PRAYER

God, help me to be a friend who listens and understands. May I show kindness and support, creating a safe space for those around me. Guide my words and actions so they reflect Your love.

Your presence can be the shelter someone needs in a storm.

JULY 28

GOD IS WITH ME EVERYWHERE

Where can I go from your Spirit? Where can I flee from your presence? If I go up to the heavens, you are there; if I make my bed in the depths, you are there. If I rise on the wings of the dawn, if I settle on the far side of the sea, even there your hand will guide me, your right hand will hold me fast.
Psalm 139:7-10

DEVOTIONAL

No matter where you are or what you're facing, you can always count on God's presence to guide and comfort you.

What are some moments in your day when you feel alone, and how can remembering that God is with you change how you approach those times?

PRAYER

Dear God, thank You for being with me everywhere I go. Help me to remember Your presence in my life, especially when I feel lonely or unsure. Amen.

Even in the toughest moments, remember—you're never alone; God is right by your side.

WHO GOD SAYS I AM

No, in all these things we are more than conquerors through him who loved us. **Romans 8:37**

DEVOTIONAL

When you learn to see yourself through God's eyes, you discover your true strength and identity, no matter the challenges you face.

What do you believe God thinks about you, and how does that shape the way you see yourself?

PRAYER

Dear God, thank you for always seeing the best in me. Help me to embrace who You say I am and to walk in confidence knowing I am loved and chosen by You.

> You are not defined by your mistakes; you are defined by God's love and purpose for you.

MADE FOR A PURPOSE

"Everyone who is called by my name, whom I created for my glory, whom I formed and made." **Isaiah 43:7**

DEVOTIONAL

You are uniquely crafted with interests and talents for a reason, so embrace that purpose and let it shine in the world around you.

What do you think your unique talents and interests reveal about the purpose God has for your life? How can you start exploring those gifts today?

PRAYER

God, thank you for creating me with a purpose. Help me to see my strengths and my passions as clues to the plans you have for me. Guide me as I seek to understand your unique calling for my life.

> Your life is a canvas, and every talent is a brushstroke that adds depth and color to your purpose.

STRENGTH IN WEAKNESS

That is why, for Christ's sake, I delight in weaknesses, in insults, in hardships, in persecutions, in difficulties. For when I am weak, then I am strong.
2 Corinthians 12:10

DEVOTIONAL

This might sound weird, but think about it: sometimes it's when we feel low or when we mess up that we can actually find real strength deep inside us. It's like getting knocked down in a game and yet coming back even better. Embracing your weaknesses can unlock a strength you never knew you had.

What are some areas in your life where you feel weak or unsure? How can you see those moments as opportunities for growth and strength instead of viewing them as failures?

PRAYER

Dear God, thank You for loving us just as we are. Help me to discover Your strength in my weaknesses and to trust that You are always there for me, guiding me through every challenge.

True strength is not the absence of weakness, but the embrace of it as a path to greater resilience.

AUGUST 1

LOVED NO MATTER WHAT

This is how God showed his love among us: He sent his one and only Son into the world that we might live through him. This is love: not that we loved God, but that he loved us and sent his Son as an atoning sacrifice for our sins.
1 John 4:9-10

DEVOTIONAL

You are loved and valued for who you are, not for what you do or achieve.

What are some moments in your life when you've felt unworthy of love, and how can you remember that you are still deeply loved in those times?

PRAYER

Dear God, thank you for loving me no matter what I face. Help me to embrace this love and share it with others, even when I'm going through tough times.

You are loved for who you are, not for what you achieve or how you perform.

AUGUST 2

MY FAITH IS MY OWN

Then Jesus told him, "Because you have seen me, you have believed; blessed are those who have not seen and yet have believed." **John 20:29**

DEVOTIONAL

Your faith is personal; it's something you cultivate in your heart, and standing firm in it can lead you to a deeper understanding of who you are.

What does it mean for you to say "my faith" rather than just following what others believe? How can you make your faith personal and unique to you? What steps can you take to explore and deepen your relationship with God?

PRAYER

Dear God, help me to embrace my faith as my own, seeking your guidance in every step I take. Give me courage to ask questions, explore new ideas, and grow closer to you each day.

Faith is not just a tradition; it's a living relationship that shapes who you are.

AUGUST 3

JESUS: MY ROLE MODEL

Whoever claims to live in him must live as Jesus did. **1 John 2:6**

DEVOTIONAL

The way you treat others shows who you are; be like Jesus and lead by example.

What qualities do you admire in Jesus, and how can you apply them to your own life as you navigate school, friendships, and challenges?

PRAYER

Dear God, thank you for sending Jesus as the ultimate role model. Help me to reflect His love, kindness, and strength in my daily life as I seek to become more like Him.

To follow Jesus is to embody love, courage, and authenticity in every step you take.

AUGUST 4

I'M A WORK IN PROGRESS

The one who calls you is faithful, and he will do it. **1 Thessalonians 5:24**

DEVOTIONAL

Remember, it's okay to be in progress; every mistake is just a stepping stone to who you're meant to be.

What areas of your life feel like they need a bit more work or growth? How can you embrace your journey as a continuous process of becoming better and stronger?

PRAYER

Dear God, thank you for being patient with me as I navigate through life. Help me to see every challenge as a step towards becoming who you want me to be. Amen.

Embracing the journey means understanding that every step, no matter how small, contributes to the masterpiece you're becoming.

CREATED ON PURPOSE

The purposes of a person's heart are deep waters, but one who has insight draws them out. **Proverbs 20:5**

DEVOTIONAL

You are created with unique interests and talents that can come together for a reason bigger than you can imagine.

What unique talents, passions, or interests has God given you that you can use to make a difference in your world? Take a moment to think about how these gifts reflect your purpose.

PRAYER

Dear God, thank You for creating me with a purpose. Help me to see what makes me unique and to use my gifts to honor You and serve others.

Every part of who you are is a piece of the masterpiece God designed.

BELONGING TO GOD

Come near to God and he will come near to you. Wash your hands, you sinners, and purify your hearts, you double-minded. **James 4:8**

DEVOTIONAL

You have a unique identity and place in God's family, which gives you a sense of belonging that no friend group can provide.

What does it mean to you to belong to God? How might that understanding change the way you see yourself and your place in the world?

PRAYER

Dear God, thank You for reminding me that I am yours. Help me to embrace my identity in You and to share Your love with those around me.

You are more than just a name; you are a child of the King.

STANDING OUT, NOT BLENDING IN

"You are the light of the world. A town built on a hill cannot be hidden."
Matthew 5:14

DEVOTIONAL

Being unique and authentic is your greatest strength;
don't be afraid to stand out.

What makes you unique, and how can you showcase your individuality in a world that often pressures you to fit in? Think about a time when you felt like you were just going with the crowd. What would it look like to choose a different path?

PRAYER

Dear God, thank You for creating me with unique gifts and talents. Help me to embrace who I truly am and give me the courage to stand out for You. May I shine brightly in my school and community as a reflection of Your love.

True strength lies in being authentically yourself.

DOING WHAT'S RIGHT WHEN NO ONE SEES

For God will bring every deed into judgment, including every hidden thing, whether it is good or evil. **Ecclesiastes 12:14**

DEVOTIONAL

Staying true to your values in the moments no one sees
shapes who you are becoming.

What does it mean to you to do what's right, even when no one is watching? Can you think of a time when you made a choice based on your values, even if it was difficult or no one else would know?

PRAYER

Dear God, help me to choose what is right, even when it feels hard or nobody is watching. Give me strength and courage to follow my heart and live authentically.

Integrity is doing the right thing, even when no one is looking.

BEING HONEST IN ALL THINGS

Therefore each of you must put off falsehood and speak truthfully to your neighbor, for we are all members of one body. **Ephesians 4:25**

DEVOTIONAL

Being honest opens doors to trust and strengthens your character, so always choose the truth, even when it's hard. Being honest isn't just about telling the truth; it's about building real connections with those around you.

What does honesty look like in your everyday life? Are there areas where you feel tempted to hide the truth or bend it just a little? Take a moment to think about how being truthful can impact your relationships and how you see yourself.

PRAYER

Dear God, help me to embrace honesty in all aspects of my life. Give me the courage to face the truth, even when it's hard, and guide me to be genuine in my words and actions.

Honesty is the foundation of true friendship and self-respect.

MY WORD MATTERS

The tongue has the power of life and death, and those who love it will eat its fruit. **Proverbs 18:21**

DEVOTIONAL

Your words can make a huge difference in someone's life, so choose them wisely and use them to build others up.

What words are you speaking to yourself and others every day? How do those words reflect who you are and what you believe about yourself?

PRAYER

God, thank You for the power of words. Help me to use my words to build up and encourage myself and those around me. May my words reflect Your love and truth.

Your words have the power to create, inspire, and uplift.

COURAGE IN EVERYDAY LIFE

The Lord is my light and my salvation—whom shall I fear? The Lord is the stronghold of my life—of whom shall I be afraid? **Psalm 27:1**

DEVOTIONAL

Sometimes, courage is simply daring to take that first step, even if you're nervous about where it might lead. Remember, having courage means trusting that you've got what it takes, even when things get tough.

What does courage mean to you in your daily life? Can you think of a specific situation recently where you felt challenged to stand up for what you believe or to push through a fear?

PRAYER

Dear God, help me to recognize the moments of bravery in my life. Grant me the strength and wisdom to face my fears and to act with kindness and integrity. Thank you for always being by my side.

Courage isn't the absence of fear; it's the decision to move forward despite it.

AUGUST 12

RESISTING PEER PRESSURE

Submit yourselves, then, to God. Resist the devil, and he will flee from you. **James 4:7**

DEVOTIONAL

When you stick to your values, you might find that others are walking beside you in the same decision. This verse reminds us that standing your ground isn't about being tough; it's about trusting in God's strength when the pressure is on.

What situations have you faced where you felt pressured to go along with the crowd, even if it didn't feel right to you? How did you respond, and what could you do differently next time?

PRAYER

Dear God, help me stand firm and be true to myself, even when others try to sway me. Grant me strength to choose what's right and the wisdom to know the difference.

True strength isn't just about resisting temptation, but about knowing who you are and living that truth boldly.

PRACTICING SELF-CONTROL

Do not be quickly provoked in your spirit, for anger resides in the lap of fools.
Ecclesiastes 7:9

DEVOTIONAL

Remember, self-control isn't just about holding back; it's about choosing to respond wisely instead of reacting in the heat of the moment.

What areas in your life do you find most challenging when it comes to self-control? Think about the choices you face daily and how they affect your goals and relationships.

PRAYER

Dear God, help me to find strength in moments of temptation. Teach me to practice self-control and remind me that I can rely on You when I feel weak.

Self-control is the key that unlocks the door to your best life.

OWNING MY MISTAKES

"Therefore, if you are offering your gift at the altar and there remember that your brother or sister has something against you, leave your gift there in front of the altar. First go and be reconciled to them; then come and offer your gift." **Matthew 5:23-24**

DEVOTIONAL

Owning up to your mistakes not only shows maturity but can also strengthen your relationships and build respect among your peers. When you take responsibility for your actions, you create an opportunity for growth and deeper connections with those around you.

What's one mistake you've made recently that you've tried to avoid owning up to? How could acknowledging it change your situation or relationship with others?

PRAYER

God, help me to embrace my mistakes and learn from them. Give me the courage to take responsibility, knowing that it leads me closer to you and to the person I want to be. Amen.

Owning your mistakes is the first step in becoming the person you're meant to be.

CHOOSING HUMILITY

Before a downfall the heart is haughty, but humility comes before honor.
Proverbs 18:12

DEVOTIONAL

Choosing humility might just be the move that turns great moments into unforgettable memories while building stronger relationships.

What does it look like for you to choose humility in your life, especially with your friends or on social media? Are there moments where you feel the pressure to show off or prove yourself instead of being authentic and grounded?

PRAYER

Father, help me to embrace humility in my daily interactions. Teach me to find strength in being humble and to reflect Your love through my actions. Amen.

True strength lies in knowing when to lift others up instead of lifting yourself.

WALKING THE TALK

Even small children are known by their actions, so is their conduct really pure and upright? **Proverbs 20:11**

DEVOTIONAL

You can talk about your values and beliefs, but what really matters is how you live them out in your actions.

What does it mean to you to live out your beliefs in your everyday actions? Can you think of a time when you 'walked the talk' or struggled to do so?

PRAYER

God, help me to align my actions with my words. Strengthen my heart to live out my faith boldly and consistently every day. May I reflect Your love in all I do.

Your actions speak so loudly, others can't hear your words.

GROWING IN GRIT

Not only so, but we also glory in our sufferings, because we know that suffering produces perseverance; perseverance, character; and character, hope. **Romans 5:3-4**

DEVOTIONAL

The struggles you face are not just obstacles; they're opportunities to build your grit and discover your true potential.

What challenges are you facing right now that require you to dig deep and show some grit? How can you take small steps today to push through these obstacles?

PRAYER

God, help me to embrace the tough times and find strength in perseverance. Teach me to trust in Your plan as I work to overcome my struggles. Amen.

> Strength doesn't come from what you can do; it comes from overcoming the things you once thought you couldn't.

EVERY CHOICE MATTERS

This day I call the heavens and the earth as witnesses against you that I have set before you life and death, blessings and curses. Now choose life, so that you and your children may live. **Deuteronomy 30:19**

DEVOTIONAL

Every choice you make today has the power to shape your tomorrow, so choose wisely and stand strong in what you believe.

What choices are you making today that might seem small but could lead to something bigger tomorrow? How do you think your decisions impact not only your life but also the lives of those around you?

PRAYER

God, help me to see the significance in my choices today. Guide my heart as I navigate through decisions, big and small, so that I can honor You and those in my life.

> Every choice is a stepping stone; some lead to paths of light, while others may lead us off course.

AUGUST 19

LEARNING FROM FAILURE

The Lord makes firm the steps of the one who delights in him; though he may stumble, he will not fall, for the Lord upholds him with his hand.
Psalm 37:23-24

DEVOTIONAL

It's a powerful reminder that even when we mess up, we're never alone. Every setback is an opportunity for a comeback; let your failures teach you how to rise stronger.

What's a recent failure you've experienced, and what lessons do you believe it could teach you about yourself or your goals?

PRAYER

Lord, help me to see my failures not as dead ends, but as opportunities for growth. Teach me to find strength in my struggles and courage to keep moving forward. Amen.

Failure is not the opposite of success; it's part of the journey.

AUGUST 20

SAYING NO WITH CONFIDENCE

"Do not let your hearts be troubled. You believe in God; believe also in me."
John 14:1

DEVOTIONAL

When you say no confidently, you express your values and boundaries. Stand firm in your decisions, and remember that who you are matters more than fitting in with the crowd.

What are some situations where you feel pressure to say yes, even when you want to say no? How can saying no help you stand strong in your beliefs and values?

PRAYER

Dear God, help me to find the courage to say no when I need to. Give me strength and wisdom in those moments, so I can stand firm in my choices and trust in Your guidance.

Saying no is not just a word; it's a way of saying yes to your own values and beliefs.

AUGUST 21

BEING A LEADER, NOT A FOLLOWER

Be on your guard; stand firm in the faith; be courageous; be strong.
1 Corinthians 16:13

DEVOTIONAL
Choose your path wisely, and remember that true leadership means having strength in your convictions, even when it's tough.

What does being a leader mean to you? Think about a time when you were faced with a decision—did you go along with what everyone else was doing, or did you stand up and make your own choice? Reflect on how your actions can influence those around you.

PRAYER
God, thank you for the strength to stand firm in who I am. Help me to be a leader who influences others in positive ways and follows your guidance in all that I do. Amen.

Saying no is not just a word; it's a way of saying yes to your own values and beliefs.

AUGUST 22

MAKING WISE FRIENDS

Walk with the wise and become wise, for a companion of fools suffers harm.
Proverbs 13:20

DEVOTIONAL
Choose friends who inspire you to be better, not those who drag you down.

What qualities do you look for in a friend, and how do those qualities reflect your own values and goals in life?

PRAYER
Dear God, help me to choose friends who uplift and inspire me. Guide me to those who encourage me in my faith and bring out the best in me. Thank you for the relationships I have and for the ones yet to come.

True leadership begins not by following the crowd, but by knowing your own direction.

MEDIA & MUSIC INFLUENCE

Those who walk righteously and speak what is right, who reject gain from extortion and keep their hands from accepting bribes, who stop their ears against plots of murder and shut their eyes against contemplating evil—they are the ones who will dwell on the heights, whose refuge will be the mountain fortress. Their bread will be supplied, and water will not fail them.
Isaiah 33:15-16

DEVOTIONAL

Don't let the media and music shape your heart; choose what uplifts and guides you instead.

PRAYER

What songs or shows do you listen to or watch that impact how you feel about yourself and the world around you? How do they shape your values, and are they pushing you towards positivity or negativity?

God, thank you for the gift of music and media. Help me to be mindful of what I fill my mind and heart with, and guide me to choose what uplifts and inspires me.

True friendship is like a treasure map; it leads you to the best parts of yourself.

AUGUST 24

WHEN THINGS DON'T GO MY WAY

In their hearts humans plan their course, but the Lord establishes their steps.
Proverbs 16:9

DEVOTIONAL

Life isn't always about you getting what you want; sometimes it's about playing your part in someone else's success.

What do you do when your plans don't work out? How do you respond when life takes an unexpected turn, and you feel like things are slipping out of your control?

PRAYER

God, help me to trust you when my plans fall apart. Guide my heart to find peace in uncertainty and remind me of the lessons you want me to learn through it all.

Your playlist can shape your path; choose tracks that lead you closer to who you're meant to be.

THINKING BEFORE I POST

Let your conversation be always full of grace, seasoned with salt, so that you may know how to answer everyone. **Colossians 4:6**

DEVOTIONAL

Think before you post; your words have the power to uplift or hurt, so choose wisely.

What are the emotions or thoughts that drive you to post something online, and have you ever thought about how it might affect someone else when you hit that "send" button?

PRAYER

Hey God, help me to be wise with my words and my actions online. Teach me to pause and consider my impact on others before I share anything. Amen.

Sometimes the detours lead to the most beautiful destinations.

CHOOSING THE HARD RIGHT

No discipline seems pleasant at the time, but painful. Later on, however, it produces a harvest of righteousness and peace for those who have been trained by it. **Hebrews 12:11**

DEVOTIONAL

The road to becoming who you want to be is often paved with tough choices, but those choices can lead to something great.

What's a recent situation where you felt torn between doing what's easy and what's right? How did you respond, and what might you do differently next time?

PRAYER

God, help me to have the courage to choose what's right, even when it's tough. Guide my heart and mind so I can stand strong and be a light to those around me. Amen.

Words can be like arrows; once they're released, you can't take them back.

GUARDING WHAT I WATCH

I will not look with approval on anything that is vile. I hate what faithless people do; I will have no part in it. **Psalm 101:3**

DEVOTIONAL

Be mindful of what you consume, as it shapes who you are and how you feel.

What do you watch, and how does it shape your thoughts, feelings, and actions? Take a moment to think about the movies, shows, and videos you consume; are they building you up or tearing you down?

PRAYER

God, help me be mindful of what I choose to watch. Let my entertainment inspire me to grow in faith and character, and guide me to focus on things that honor You. Amen.

The hard right is always better than the easy wrong.

MANAGING ANGER

Fools give full vent to their rage, but the wise bring calm in the end. **Proverbs 29:11**

DEVOTIONAL

Anger can flare up quickly, but it's how you handle it that can define who you are.

What makes you feel angry, and how do you usually respond? Take a moment to think about a time when you felt that fire rising inside you. How could you handle that situation differently next time?

PRAYER

God, help me to understand my anger and guide me in expressing it constructively. Teach me patience and wisdom, so I can respond with grace in challenging moments. Amen.

Your eyes are windows to your soul; guard them carefully.

AUGUST 29

WHEN I FEEL ALONE

I will not leave you as orphans; I will come to you. **John 14:18**

DEVOTIONAL
When you feel alone, remember that sometimes connection starts with the courage to reach out to someone else.

What are some moments when you feel most alone, and how do they make you see yourself and others?

PRAYER
God, thank you for always being with me, even when I feel lonely. Help me to remember that I am never truly alone and to reach out for connection when I need it.

"Anger is like a fire; it can either warm you or burn you."

AUGUST 30

DEALING WITH STRESS

Anxiety weighs down the heart, but a kind word cheers it up. **Proverbs 12:25**

DEVOTIONAL
When stress feels overwhelming, remember that sharing it with God can lighten your load and put things in perspective.

What stresses you out the most right now, and how can you take a moment to breathe and find peace in the midst of it?

PRAYER
God, thank You for being with me through every challenge. Help me to lean on Your strength when stress feels overwhelming, and remind me to take things one step at a time.

In the silence of your loneliness, God whispers that you are never truly by yourself.

GOD IN MY ANXIETY

When anxiety was great within me, your consolation brought me joy.
Psalm 94:19

DEVOTIONAL
The more you talk to God about your anxiety, the more you'll realize we're never meant to face our struggles alone.

What are some situations where you've felt anxious, and how can you invite God into those moments to find peace?

PRAYER
God, when anxiety feels overwhelming, remind me that I am not alone. Help me to trust in Your presence and find calm in the chaos. Amen.

In the middle of chaos, peace is still possible.

DID THIS DEVOTIONAL MAKE A DIFFERENCE?

Hey Brother,

If these daily devotionals have helped you grow in confidence, courage, or faith, I'd be grateful if you shared your experience with others.

Your review on Amazon can help more teen boys discover this book and start their own journey toward a stronger faith and purpose.

To leave your review, just scan the QR code below with your phone's camera, or type the link into your computer or phone's browser.

https://go.binnovatedigital.com/TeenBoysDevotional

HANDLING DISAPPOINTMENT

But the one who stands firm to the end will be saved. **Matthew 24:13**

DEVOTIONAL

Disappointment is just a stepping stone to greater things; how you respond makes all the difference.

What disappointments have you faced recently, and how did they make you feel? How can you view these setbacks as opportunities for growth instead of failure?

PRAYER

Dear God, help me to understand that disappointments are part of life. Teach me to lean on You during those tough times and to find strength in my challenges. Amen.

Even in my most anxious moments, God is my anchor.

FIGHTING NEGATIVE THOUGHTS

You, dear children, are from God and have overcome them, because the one who is in you is greater than the one who is in the world. **1 John 4:4**

DEVOTIONAL

Believe in yourself and remember, it's not about being better than anyone else; it's about embracing who you really are.

What negative thoughts have been creeping into your mind lately? How do you usually react when those thoughts come up, and what would it look like to challenge them instead?

PRAYER

God, help me to recognize my negative thoughts and find strength in You. Replace my doubts with confidence and my fears with courage as I navigate this journey of life. Amen.

Disappointment is not the end but a stepping stone to something greater.

BUILDING CONFIDENCE

For the Lord will be at your side and will keep your foot from being snared.
Proverbs 3:26

DEVOTIONAL

Believe in the skills and preparation you've worked hard to build; they're your true support when you're feeling uncertain.

What are some strengths or talents you have that you sometimes overlook or underestimate in yourself? How can you celebrate those parts of who you are?

PRAYER

God, thank you for the unique gifts and talents you've given me. Help me to recognize my worth and build my confidence in you. May I find courage in every step I take.

Your mind is a battlefield; choose your battles wisely.

WHEN I'M SAD

A cheerful heart is good medicine, but a crushed spirit dries up the bones.
Proverbs 17:22

DEVOTIONAL

When you're feeling sad, remember that sharing your struggles with someone can lighten your load and bring back your joy.

What are some things that make you feel sad, and how can you share those feelings with someone who cares?

PRAYER

Dear God, when I feel sad, help me to remember that I'm not alone. Surround me with your love and guide me to those who can lift my spirit.

Confidence grows when we recognize and affirm the greatness within us.

FINDING PEACE

You will keep in perfect peace those whose minds are steadfast, because they trust in you. **Isaiah 26:3**

DEVOTIONAL
You can find peace within yourself by trusting in your abilities and focusing on what truly matters.

What does peace look like for you in the midst of your daily challenges? When have you felt a moment of true calm, and how can you seek more of that in your life?

PRAYER
God, thank You for being the source of true peace. Help me to trust You in every situation and to find solace in Your presence, especially when life feels overwhelming.

Peace isn't the absence of trouble; it's the presence of God in the middle of it.

SPENDING MONEY WISELY

The wise store up choice food and olive oil, but fools gulp theirs down. **Proverbs 21:20**

DEVOTIONAL
Think before you spend; deciding what truly enhances your life is smarter than buying on impulse.

What are some of the things you spend your money on, and how do those choices reflect what's truly important to you?

PRAYER
Dear God, help me to make wise choices with my money. Give me the wisdom to know what I truly need and the strength to resist what I don't. I want to honor You with the way I use my resources.

True wealth is not measured by how much you have, but by how wisely you use what you possess.

BEING A LOYAL FRIEND

Greater love has no one than this: to lay down one's life for one's friends.
John 15:13

DEVOTIONAL
Always be the kind of friend who shows up, especially when it's tough.

What does loyalty as a friend look like in your life? Can you think of a time when you stood by a friend or when you needed someone to stand by you? How did that shape your friendship?

PRAYER
God, thank You for the gift of friendship. Help me to be a loyal friend who encourages and supports those around me. Grant me the wisdom to know how to stand by others, just as You stand by me.

True friendship is not just about being there for someone;
it's about being there for them when it matters the most.

FORGIVING OTHERS

Whoever would foster love covers over an offense, but whoever repeats the matter separates close friends. **Proverbs 17:9**

DEVOTIONAL
True friendship means having each other's backs and offering forgiveness when life gets messy.

What do you find most difficult about forgiving someone who has hurt you? How can letting go of that hurt change your perspective and your relationships?

PRAYER
Dear God, help me to open my heart and give me the strength to forgive those who have wronged me. May I find peace in letting go of resentment and embrace the healing that comes with forgiveness.

Forgiveness is a gift you give yourself, allowing you to move
forward without the weight of anger.

WHEN FRIENDS HURT YOU

Wounds from a friend can be trusted, but an enemy multiplies kisses.
Proverbs 27:6

DEVOTIONAL

People aren't perfect, and friendships will have ups and downs; don't let the hurt define you—learn to lean into God for healing and wisdom.

What's a recent experience where a friend's words or actions hurt you, and how did you respond?

PRAYER

Dear God, please help me to heal from the hurt caused by my friends. Teach me how to forgive and guide me in understanding their actions. Surround me with your love and strength.

> True friendship can sometimes be messy, but through the mess, we learn more about grace and healing.

RESPECTING MY PARENTS

Listen, my son, to your father's instruction and do not forsake your mother's teaching. **Proverbs 1:8**

DEVOTIONAL

Respecting your parents isn't just about obedience; it's about recognizing the value of their life lessons and the love behind their guidance.

What do you think it means to truly respect your parents, even when you don't agree with them? How can you show them kindness and understanding in your day-to-day interactions?

PRAYER

Dear God, help me to see my parents through Your eyes. Teach me to honor them with my words and actions, even when things get tough. Thank you for their love and guidance in my life.

> Respect is the bridge that connects love and understanding.

SIBLING STRUGGLES

Do to others as you would have them do to you. **Luke 6:31**

DEVOTIONAL

In the heat of sibling struggles, remember that love for family can often conquer fleeting anger and pride.

What are some ways you can be a better brother, even when you feel annoyed or misunderstood by your sibling?

PRAYER

Dear God, thank You for my siblings, even when it's hard to get along. Help me to show patience and love, and to see things from their perspective.

Love is not just a feeling; it's a choice we make every day.

SEPTEMBER 12

BEING A PEACEMAKER

Let the peace of Christ rule in your hearts, since as members of one body you were called to peace. And be thankful. **Colossians 3:15**

DEVOTIONAL

Being a peacemaker in tough situations makes you a true leader and a friend others can rely on.

What does being a peacemaker look like in your life? Can you think of a situation where you could bring calm instead of conflict?

PRAYER

God, please help me to be a source of peace in my relationships. Teach me to speak and act with kindness, especially when things get tough. Thank you for your guidance in my heart.

Peacemaking starts with understanding, not just being understood.

SEPTEMBER 13

CHOOSING FRIENDS WISELY

"If the world hates you, keep in mind that it hated me first. If you belonged to the world, it would love you as its own. As it is, you do not belong to the world, but I have chosen you out of the world. That is why the world hates you.
John 15:18-19

DEVOTIONAL
Sometimes, feeling left out can be an invitation to find deeper, more meaningful connections.

What memories come to mind when you felt left out? How did those experiences affect your self-worth and relationships with others? Take a moment to think about how they shaped your perspective.

PRAYER
Dear God, help me to remember that I am never truly alone, even when it feels like it. Fill my heart with your love and remind me of my value in your eyes. Amen.

> Feeling left out can open the door to discovering your true self and finding those who truly value you.

SEPTEMBER 14

WHEN I FEEL LEFT OUT

Two are better than one, because they have a good return for their labor: If either of them falls down, one can help the other up. But pity anyone who falls and has no one to help them up. **Ecclesiastes 4:9-10**

DEVOTIONAL
You have the power to uplift those around you; your godly influence can make a real difference in someone's life.

What kind of influence do you think you have on your friends? How do your choices reflect your values and your faith?

PRAYER
Dear God, thank you for the people in our lives who inspire us. Help me be a positive influence to those around me, reflecting your love and truth in all I do.

> Your life is the message; make it worth hearing.

GODLY INFLUENCE

After David had finished talking with Saul, Jonathan became one in spirit with David, and he loved him as himself. **1 Samuel 18:1**

DEVOTIONAL

Sometimes friendship breakups hurt, but they can lead you to understand yourself better and make room for relationships that build you up.

What does it feel like when a friendship ends, and how does it change the way you see yourself and those around you? Reflect on the emotions you experienced and how you can heal from the loss.

PRAYER

God, thank you for the friends you've brought into my life. Help me to navigate the pain of losing a friendship, and remind me that I am never alone in this journey.

Sometimes, a friendship ends so that you can grow into the person you're meant to be.

SEPTEMBER 16

FRIENDSHIP BREAKUPS

But when you pray, go into your room, close the door and pray to your Father, who is unseen. Then your Father, who sees what is done in secret, will reward you. **Matthew 6:6**

DEVOTIONAL

Sometimes, stepping away from the chaos to have an honest conversation with God can bring clarity and peace you didn't know you needed.

What does prayer mean to you, and how can it help you navigate the challenges you're facing right now? Take a moment to think about the things you want to share with God.

PRAYER

Hey God, thank You for always being there for me. Help me to be open and honest in my prayers, and remind me that I'm never alone in my struggles.

Prayer is not just a routine; it's a relationship.

HOW TO PRAY

And we also thank God continually because, when you received the word of God, which you heard from us, you accepted it not as a human word, but as it actually is, the word of God, which is indeed at work in you who believe.

1 Thessalonians 2:13

DEVOTIONAL

In the chaos of everyday life, taking even a few moments to read the Bible can provide direction and strength, reminding us that we're never alone in our struggles.

What would change in your life if you made reading the Bible a daily habit? How do you think it could help you navigate school, friendships, and even the challenges you face as a teen?

PRAYER

Dear God, thank You for giving us Your Word. Help me to make time each day to connect with You through the Bible, growing in my faith and understanding. Amen.

Daily moments with God can transform ordinary days into extraordinary ones.

READING THE BIBLE DAILY

For the word of God is alive and active. Sharper than any double-edged sword, it penetrates even to dividing soul and spirit, joints and marrow; it judges the thoughts and attitudes of the heart. **Hebrews 4:12**

DEVOTIONAL

When you fill your mind with God's Word, you equip yourself with strength and guidance for whatever life throws your way.

What do you think would change in your life if you made memorizing God's Word a priority this week? How might it help you face challenges or temptations?

PRAYER

Dear God, thank You for the gift of Your Word. Help me to remember its truths and let them guide my thoughts and actions each day. Give me the strength and motivation to commit these verses to memory.

God's Word is not just for reading; it's meant to become a part of you.

MEMORIZING GOD'S WORD

As the deer pants for streams of water, so my soul pants for you, my God. My soul thirsts for God, for the living God. When can I go and meet with God?
Psalm 42:1-2

DEVOTIONAL

Just because you can't feel God or see Him right now doesn't mean He isn't right beside you, waiting for you to reach out.

What's one time when you felt God was distant from you, and how did that affect your faith?

PRAYER

Dear God, even when we feel alone, help us to remember Your presence is always near. Open our hearts to seek You during those tough times and fill us with reassurance of Your love.

Even in silence, God is working behind the scenes.

SEPTEMBER 20

WORSHIP WITH MY LIFE

Through Jesus, therefore, let us continually offer to God a sacrifice of praise—the fruit of lips that openly profess his name. And do not forget to do good and to share with others, for with such sacrifices God is pleased.
Hebrews 13:15-16

DEVOTIONAL

Worship isn't just about the songs we sing; it's how we show up for others and live out our faith every day.

What does it mean for you to worship God with your life every day, in the little moments and the big decisions? How can you express your faith in the way you treat others and live out your passions?

PRAYER

Lord, help me to see each day as an opportunity to live my life as an act of worship. Guide my choices and actions so that they reflect Your love and grace, in everything I do. Amen.

Worship isn't just a song; it's a way of living that shows who we are and who we belong to.

SEPTEMBER 21

WHAT IS QUIET TIME?

"I am the vine; you are the branches. If you remain in me and I in you, you will bear much fruit; apart from me you can do nothing. **John 15:5**

DEVOTIONAL

Making quiet time a habit helps you tap into His strength and wisdom, allowing you to grow and thrive, just like the branches that flourish when they're connected to the vine.

What does "quiet time" mean to you, and how can setting aside time each day help you deepen your relationship with God? Imagine the impact of starting or ending your day with intention and focus.

PRAYER

Dear God, thank you for the moments of stillness in our lives. Help me to find and cherish these times, so I can hear your voice and grow closer to you. Amen.

Quiet time is not just about the absence of noise; it's about creating space for God's presence.

SEPTEMBER 22

TRUSTING GOD'S TIMING

He has made everything beautiful in its time. He has also set eternity in the human heart; yet no one can fathom what God has done from beginning to end. **Ecclesiastes 3:11**

DEVOTIONAL

Timing can feel frustrating, but know that what's meant for you will arrive just when it's supposed to—stay focused and keep grinding.

What does it feel like when you have to wait for something you really want? Can you recall a time when you had to trust that things would work out in their own time?

PRAYER

Dear God, thank you for your constant presence in my life. Help me to trust your timing in everything, even when it feels hard. I know good things come in your perfect timing.

Patience isn't just about waiting; it's about trusting that what you're waiting for is worth it.

ASKING GOD FOR GUIDANCE

But the Advocate, the Holy Spirit, whom the Father will send in my name, will teach you all things and will remind you of everything I have said to you.
John 14:26

DEVOTIONAL

It's like having a coach by your side, guiding you through tough plays and tough decisions. When you ask God for guidance in your decisions, trust that He's got your back and will point you in the right direction.

What do you really need help with right now, and how might asking God for guidance change your perspective on it?

PRAYER

God, I come to You with an open heart, seeking Your direction in my life. Please guide me through the choices I face, and help me to trust in Your wisdom and plan for me. Thank You for always being there, ready to listen.

Sometimes the bravest thing we can do is ask for help on the path we're meant to take.

SEPTEMBER 24

LISTENING TO GOD

My sheep listen to my voice; I know them, and they follow me. **John 10:27**

DEVOTIONAL

When you choose to listen for God in the silence, you discover His guidance amidst your daily chaos.

What are some of the distractions in your life that make it hard to hear what God is saying to you? How can you create space for His voice?

PRAYER

God, help me to quiet my heart and open my ears so I can hear You through the noise around me. Teach me to seek Your direction and wisdom each day.

Listening to God is the first step in understanding His purpose for your life.

FASTING: WHAT AND WHY?

If you find honey, eat just enough—too much of it, and you will vomit.
Proverbs 25:16

DEVOTIONAL
Fasting isn't about going hungry; it's about making space for something greater in your life. Take a moment to think about what distracts you the most, and consider giving it up to grow closer to God.

What does fasting mean to you, and how do you think it could bring you closer to God? Have you ever considered what distractions in your life might take your focus away from Him?

PRAYER
God, help me understand the purpose of fasting and give me the strength to embrace it as a way to grow closer to You. Show me how to replace distractions with deeper devotion.

Fasting isn't just about giving something up; it's about making space for something greater.

FAITH OVER FEELINGS

It is better to take refuge in the Lord than to trust in humans. **Psalm 118:8**

DEVOTIONAL
When your feelings try to take control, remember that trusting in God's plan is always a better play.

What feelings are you facing today that might be trying to steer your decisions? Can you think of a time when choosing faith over those feelings made a positive impact in your life?

PRAYER
Dear God, help me to remember that my feelings are not always truth. Strengthen my faith so that I can trust Your guidance and love, even when my emotions are all over the place.

Faith is the compass that leads us through the storm of our feelings.

STANDING UP FOR WHAT'S RIGHT

Stand firm then, with the belt of truth buckled around your waist, with the breastplate of righteousness in place. **Ephesians 6:14**

DEVOTIONAL

Choosing to stand up for what is right can be tough, but it builds your character and shows others that you care.

What does standing up for what's right look like in your life? Can you think of a recent situation where you felt you should have spoken up or acted differently?

PRAYER

Dear God, help me to recognize the moments when I need to stand up for what is right. Give me courage and wisdom to act with integrity and kindness in those times. Amen.

Courage isn't the absence of fear, but the decision to do what is right, even when it's hard.

BEING DIFFERENT FOR A REASON

Each one should test their own actions. Then they can take pride in themselves alone, without comparing themselves to someone else, for each one should carry their own load. **Galatians 6:4-5**

DEVOTIONAL

Life is not about fitting into someone else's mold, but about celebrating what makes you uniquely you.

What makes you feel different from the guys around you? How can those unique qualities be used to make a positive impact in your friendships and the world?

PRAYER

Dear God, thank you for making me unique. Help me understand and embrace my differences, using them to shine your light in the world. I trust that I am created for a purpose.

Being different is not a flaw; it's a gift designed to bring change in a world that desperately needs it.

SEPTEMBER 29

SHARING MY FAITH

"Whoever acknowledges me before others, I will also acknowledge before my Father in heaven." **Matthew 10:32**

DEVOTIONAL

Sharing your faith can be as simple as being yourself and building genuine connections with others.

What does sharing your faith look like in your everyday life? How do you feel when you think about opening up about your beliefs to friends or family? Take a moment to consider the impact your story could have on someone else.

PRAYER

God, thank you for the gift of faith and the people in my life. Help me to share my beliefs with courage and kindness, so that others can see Your love through me. Amen.

Your story is a bridge that can connect hearts and open doors to faith.

SEPTEMBER 30

LEADING BY EXAMPLE

Remember your leaders, who spoke the word of God to you. Consider the outcome of their way of life and imitate their faith. **Hebrews 13:7**

DEVOTIONAL

Being a leader isn't about being the loudest voice; sometimes, it's just lifting others up with your actions.

What does it look like for you to lead by example in your daily life? Think about the way you treat your friends, handle conflicts, or stay true to your values. Can you think of a time when your actions made a positive impact on someone else?

PRAYER

God, help me to be a strong example to those around me. May my words and actions reflect Your love and truth, guiding others to see You through me. Thank You for the people who inspire me to lead with integrity.

Your actions are the bridge between your beliefs and the world around you.

OCTOBER 1

FAITH IN HARD MOMENTS

"And teaching them to obey everything I have commanded you. And surely I am with you always, to the very end of the age." **Matthew 28:20**

DEVOTIONAL

Faith isn't just for the good times; it's a lifeline during the tough moments, reminding you that you're never alone.

What hard moment in your life feels overwhelming right now? How might your faith help you navigate through it and find hope in the midst of it?

PRAYER

Dear God, help me to trust you when times are tough. Grant me the strength to see your presence in my challenges, and remind me that I am never alone in my struggles.

Faith is not the absence of fear, but the courage to trust despite it.

OCTOBER 2

WHEN I'M THE ONLY CHRISTIAN

But as for you, be strong and do not give up, for your work will be rewarded."
2 Chronicles 15:7

DEVOTIONAL

Stand firm in your beliefs, even when it feels like you're the only one doing so. Your courage can be the spark that encourages others to stand up for what they believe in too.

What does it feel like to be the only Christian in your friend group or at school? How do you navigate conversations that challenge your faith or make you feel isolated?

PRAYER

Dear God, help me stand strong in my faith when I feel alone. Give me the courage to shine Your light and show your love to others, even when it's tough.

Your faith can be a beacon, even in the darkest places.

OCTOBER 3

SPEAKING TRUTH WITH KINDNESS

Instead, speaking the truth in love, we will grow to become in every respect the mature body of him who is the head, that is, Christ. **Ephesians 4:15**

DEVOTIONAL

Always remember that being truthful is important, but wrapping it in kindness is what builds strong relationships.

What does it mean for you to speak the truth, and how can you do so in a way that shows kindness to those around you?

PRAYER

Dear God, guide us as we learn to speak truthfully while being kind. Help us to communicate with love in our hearts, even when it's hard. Thank You for always being there to support us.

Speaking truth isn't just about what you say; it's about how you say it.

OCTOBER 4

CONFIDENCE THROUGH CHRIST

Brothers and sisters, think of what you were when you were called. Not many of you were wise by human standards; not many were influential; not many were of noble birth. But God chose the foolish things of the world to shame the wise; God chose the weak things of the world to shame the strong. God chose the lowly things of this world and the despised things—and the things that are not—to nullify the things that are,
so that no one may boast before him. **1 Corinthians 1:26-29**

DEVOTIONAL

True confidence comes from realizing your value in Christ, not from what others think of you.

What situations in your life make you feel unsure of yourself? How can you invite Christ into those moments to find confidence and strength?

PRAYER

Lord, thank you for being my guide and my foundation. Help me to trust in You and find confidence in who I am because of Your love. Amen.

Your true identity and confidence come from knowing who you are in Christ.

OCTOBER 5

RISKING COMFORT FOR PURPOSE

David said to the Philistine, "You come against me with sword and spear and javelin, but I come against you in the name of the Lord Almighty, the God of the armies of Israel, whom you have defied. This day the Lord will deliver you into my hands, and I'll strike you down and cut off your head. This very day I will give the carcasses of the Philistine army to the birds and the wild animals, and the whole world will know that there is a God in Israel. All those gathered here will know that it is not by sword or spear that the Lord saves; for the battle is the Lord's, and he will give all of you into our hands." **1 Samuel 17:45-47**

DEVOTIONAL

When you choose to step out of your comfort zone for something important—like standing up for a friend, trying out for a team, or volunteering—you're not just taking a risk. You're embracing a purpose that can lead to growth and strength, just like David when he picked up that sling. Sometimes, risking your comfort can open doors that lead to your true purpose.

What does it mean for you to step out of your comfort zone to pursue bigger goals in your life? Can you think of a time when taking a risk led to something good?

PRAYER

Dear God, help me to see that true purpose often lies beyond my comfort. Give me the courage to take the steps necessary to pursue my dreams, even when it feels uncomfortable. Amen.

Stepping out of your comfort zone can lead to discovering
the purpose you were created for.

OCTOBER 6

FAITH IN PUBLIC

In everything set them an example by doing what is good. In your teaching show integrity, seriousness and soundness of speech that cannot be condemned, so that those who oppose you may be ashamed because they have nothing bad to say about us. **Titus 2:7-8**

DEVOTIONAL

The way you stand up for what's right—whether with friends, teammates, or in your daily life—can inspire others to act with integrity too. Don't be afraid to show your faith publicly; it might just encourage someone else to do the same.

What does it look like for you to live out your faith in your school or among your friends? Are there times when you feel pressure to keep your beliefs to yourself?

PRAYER

Dear God, help me to be brave in sharing my faith with those around me. Give me the wisdom to know when to speak and the courage to act with love. Thank you for standing by my side no matter where I am.

True faith shines brightest when it's shared, not hidden.

OCTOBER 7

WHY AM I HERE?

So God created mankind in his own image, in the image of God he created them; male and female he created them. **Genesis 1:27**

DEVOTIONAL

This means you're made with purpose, designed to reflect something incredible about who God is. You are here to make an impact, not just for yourself but for those around you.

What are the unique interests, talents, and dreams that you feel pull you forward in life? How do these passions reflect your identity and purpose in the world around you?

PRAYER

Dear God, thank you for creating me with a purpose. Help me to discover and embrace the unique path you have laid out for me, and guide me as I seek to understand why I'm here.

You are not an accident; you are a part of something bigger than yourself.

OCTOBER 8

WHAT GOD SAYS ABOUT SUCCESS

But seek first his kingdom and his righteousness, and all these things will be given to you as well. **Matthew 6:33**

DEVOTIONAL

True success isn't about accolades or accolades but about building others up and staying true to what matters.

What does success mean to you, and how do you think God views your journey towards it? Are you measuring your worth by grades, social status, or something deeper? Take a moment to reflect on what truly matters.

PRAYER

God, help me see success through Your eyes. Guide me in my efforts and remind me that true achievement comes from following Your path and being faithful in my work. Thank You for being my strength and my guide.

Success isn't just about what you achieve; it's about who you become in the process.

DISCOVERING MY GIFTS

"Again, it will be like a man going on a journey, who called his servants and entrusted his wealth to them. To one he gave five bags of gold, to another two bags, and to another one bag, each according to his ability. Then he went on his journey." **Matthew 25:14-15**

DEVOTIONAL

Sometimes, we may not see the gifts we have because we are too focused on what others are doing. Discovering who you are can be a journey, where your unique talents come into view when you least expect them. You have unique gifts and talents meant to make a difference; embrace them instead of comparing yourself to others.

What are some talents or interests you have that you might not fully appreciate yet? How can you explore them more deeply this week?

PRAYER

God, thank You for the unique gifts You've placed within me. Help me to recognize and embrace these talents so I can use them to shine in the world around me.

Your gifts are like stars; some shine brightly,
while others are waiting to be discovered.

DREAMING BIG WITH GOD

Jesus looked at them and said, "With man this is impossible, but with God all things are possible." **Matthew 19:26**

DEVOTIONAL

Never underestimate what you can achieve with hard work and faith—dream big, because with God, nothing is impossible.

What big dreams do you have for your life, and how do you think God might be calling you to pursue them?

PRAYER

Dear God, thank you for the dreams you place in our hearts. Help me to trust in your guidance as I seek to follow the plans you have for me. Amen.

When you dream big with God, impossible becomes possible.

OCTOBER 11

MAKING THE MOST OF MY YOUTH

Remember your Creator in the days of your youth, before the days of trouble come and the years approach when you will say, "I find no pleasure in them". **Ecclesiastes 12:1**

DEVOTIONAL

Don't let the days of your youth slip away without making the most of them; invest in your passions, relationships, and your future now.

What are the dreams or passions you have right now, and how can you take small steps to pursue them today?

PRAYER

Dear God, help me embrace this time in my life as a gift. Give me courage and wisdom to explore my passions and to make choices that honor You.

Today is the foundation upon which your future will be built.

OCTOBER 12

USING MY FREE TIME FOR GOOD

He has shown you, O mortal, what is good. And what does the Lord require of you? To act justly and to love mercy and to walk humbly with your God.
Micah 6:8

DEVOTIONAL

Make the most of your free time by choosing to invest it in others; you might be surprised at how much you grow and learn along the way.

What are some ways you can use your free time this week to make a positive impact on others around you?

PRAYER

God, thank You for the gift of time. Help me to see the opportunities around me and guide me to use my free moments to do good and uplift others.

Your time is a powerful tool; how will you choose to wield it?

LOVING GOD MORE THAN COMFORT

Whoever serves me must follow me; and where I am, my servant also will be. My Father will honor the one who serves me. **John 12:26**

DEVOTIONAL

True love for God sometimes means choosing faith over fun.

What comforts do you lean on most during tough times, and are you willing to let them go to grow closer to God?

PRAYER

God, I want to learn to love You more than my comfort. Help me to trust in You even when it feels hard, and show me how to seek Your presence instead of just what feels easy.

Sometimes our greatest growth happens when we step outside our comfort zone and embrace the unknown with faith.

NOT LETTING ANGER WIN

Be angry, and do not sin; ponder in your own hearts on your beds, and be silent. **Psalm 4:4**

DEVOTIONAL

When anger rises, take a step back, breathe, and choose to respond with grace rather than react in fury.

What situations in your life make you feel the most angry, and how can you take a step back to respond with kindness instead?

PRAYER

God, help me to recognize when anger starts to rise within me. Teach me to pause, breathe, and choose love over frustration. Fill my heart with peace and understanding, Amen.

Anger is a visitor; don't let it set up permanent residence in your heart.

PREPARING FOR MANHOOD

"Each person must bear their own load."
Galatians 6:5

DEVOTIONAL

Maturing into manhood means recognizing that your actions carry weight, and it's up to you to shape your future through the choices you make today.

What are the qualities you admire in the men around you, and how can you start embodying those traits in your own life? Think about one way you can take a step toward becoming the man you want to be.

PRAYER

Dear God, thank You for guiding me as I grow into the man You created me to be. Help me to understand the responsibilities that come with manhood and give me the strength to embrace them with courage and grace.

Being a man isn't just about age; it's about
the choices you make and the character you build.

SERVING OTHERS WITH MY TALENTS

"The generous will prosper; those who refresh others will themselves be refreshed." **Proverbs 11:25**

DEVOTIONAL

Using your talents to uplift others can create lasting bonds and incredible outcomes that lift everyone up.

What are some talents you have that could make a difference in someone else's life? How might using these gifts change how you see yourself and others?

PRAYER

God, thank You for the unique talents You've given me. Help me to use them to serve others and show Your love in my actions. Amen.

Your talents are a form of love that can light up someone else's world.

OCTOBER 17

MAKING EVERY DAY COUNT

"Teach us to make the most of our time, so we may grow in wisdom."
Psalm 90:12

DEVOTIONAL

You have the power to shape your days—don't just let them pass by; discover what you truly enjoy and grow from it.

What does it mean for you to make today count? How can you engage in something meaningful to turn an ordinary moment into an extraordinary one?

PRAYER

Dear God, help me to see the purpose in every day and embrace opportunities to grow. Guide my actions, so I can make choices that honor You and reflect Your love.

Every day is a blank canvas; paint it with the colors of your dreams and intentions.

OCTOBER 18

GAMING & SELF-CONTROL

"If your right eye causes you to stumble, gouge it out and throw it away."
Matthew 5:29-30

DEVOTIONAL

Self-control isn't about giving up what you love; it's about making room for all the greatness life has to offer.

What does gaming mean to you? How do you find balance between enjoying your favorite games and making time for other important aspects of your life, like friendships, studies, or family?

PRAYER

Dear God, help me to seek balance in my life. Grant me the strength to enjoy my gaming while also making room for the things that truly matter. Amen.

Self-control isn't just about saying 'no'—it's about knowing when to say 'yes' to what really counts.

PHONES, LIKES, AND IDENTITY

What a person desires is unfailing love; better to be poor than a liar.
Proverbs 19:22

DEVOTIONAL
Your identity isn't shaped by your phone or how many likes you get; it's rooted in who you are and the love that surrounds you.

What do you think your phone says about who you are? Is it just a tool for communication, or does it influence how you see yourself, your worth, and your relationships with others?

PRAYER
Dear God, help me to see my true identity in You, not through the lens of likes or followers. Guide me to use my phone and social media in a way that reflects Your love and truth.

Your worth is not measured by your likes, but by the love that God has for you.

HANDLING ONLINE TEMPTATION

"Blessed are the pure in heart, for they will see God."
Matthew 5:8

DEVOTIONAL
Choose what fills your heart wisely because true strength is found in saying 'no' to what harms you.

What are some moments online when you've felt tempted to do or see things you know aren't right? How did those moments make you feel, and what could you do differently next time?

PRAYER
Dear God, help me to navigate my online world with strength and wisdom. Grant me the courage to say no to temptation and the clarity to choose what honors you.

Choosing what's right online shows strength that goes beyond the screen.

PEER PRESSURE & GROUP CHATS

"You can enter God's Kingdom only through the narrow gate. The highway to destruction is broad, and its gate is wide for the many who choose that way. But the gateway to life is very narrow and the road is difficult, and only a few ever find it." **Matthew 7:13-14**

DEVOTIONAL

When it comes to peer pressure, remember that it's okay to be different; true friends will respect your choices.

What do you feel when your friends pressure you to act a certain way or say things you're uncomfortable with? How do you navigate those moments in your group chats when everyone seems to be going along with the crowd?

PRAYER

God, help me to find strength in You when I feel the weight of my friends' expectations. Remind me that true friendship means lifting each other up, not bringing each other down.

True courage is standing firm in who you are, even when it feels like everyone else is trying to pull you away.

WHEN I'M JUDGED FOR BELIEVING

"Don't be intimidated in any way by your opponents. This will be a sign to them that they are going to be destroyed, but that you are going to be saved, even by God himself." **Philippians 1:28**

DEVOTIONAL

When you stand up for your beliefs, you're not just being strong; you're showing others that it's okay to think differently.

What does it feel like when someone judges you for what you believe? How do you respond to their comments, and how does it affect your confidence in your faith?

PRAYER

God, thank You for being with me through every judgment I face. Help me to stand tall in my beliefs and remind me that Your love is greater than any criticism I encounter. Give me the strength to show grace to those who don't understand.

Your faith can be your greatest strength, even when others don't see it.

CANCEL CULTURE VS. GRACE

"Do not judge, and you will not be judged. Do not condemn, and you will not be condemned. Forgive, and you will be forgiven." **Luke 6:37**

DEVOTIONAL

In a world quick to judge and cancel those who miss the mark, remember that we all stumble and need grace.

What does it feel like to you when someone gets "canceled"? Have you ever been in a situation where you felt judged or unfairly treated? How can you extend grace to others, even those who make mistakes?

PRAYER

God, help me to be a source of grace and understanding in a world that often judges harshly. Teach me to see others through Your eyes and to offer forgiveness just as You have forgiven me. Amen.

Grace invites us to rise above the noise and be a light instead of a judge.

TOXIC MASCULINITY VS. GODLY STRENGTH

"Finally, be strong in the Lord and in His mighty power."
Ephesians 6:10

DEVOTIONAL

Real strength comes from showing compassion and being there for others, not from pretending to be tough.

What does being strong mean to you, and how can you differentiate between the strength that society values and the strength God calls you to embody?

PRAYER

God, help me to seek true strength in my life. Allow me to embrace the qualities You value—humility, love, and courage—as I navigate my understanding of masculinity.

"True strength is not measured by how hard you can hit,
but by how gently you can lift others up."

OCTOBER 25

SOCIAL MEDIA COMPARISON

"Don't be fooled. The one who thinks he is something when he is nothing is fooling himself." **Galatians 6:3**

DEVOTIONAL

Remember, social media shows a filtered version of life; it's more important to enjoy your own journey than to compare it to someone else's highlight reel.

What do you feel when you see someone else's life on social media? Do you ever find yourself wishing you had what they have, or feeling like you fall short in comparison?

PRAYER

Dear God, help me see my worth through Your eyes and not through the filtered lens of social media. Remind me to focus on the blessings and unique journey You've given me. Amen.

Your value isn't in how you compare to others,
but in how you embrace your own unique story.

OCTOBER 26

FEELING BEHIND EVERYONE ELSE

"The Lord is your strength and shield; in Him, your heart trusts, and you are helped. Your heart exults, and with your song, you give thanks." **Psalm 28:7**

DEVOTIONAL

Don't compare your journey to someone else's; it's perfectly okay to take your time and grow at your own speed.

What does it feel like when you see your friends succeeding in areas where you feel like you're lagging behind? Have you ever wondered if your journey looks different for a reason?

PRAYER

Dear God, please remind me that my path is unique and that it's okay to take my time. Help me trust in Your timing and find peace in my own progress. Amen.

Not everyone's race is the same; your pace is perfectly yours.

DEALING WITH BULLYING

"The Lord hears his people when they call to him for help. He rescues them from all their troubles. The Lord is close to the brokenhearted and rescues those whose spirits are crushed." **Psalm 34:17-19**

DEVOTIONAL

Remember, when dealing with bullying, staying true to who you are and surrounding yourself with genuine friends can help light the way through tough times.

What does it feel like when you face bullying, and how can you respond with strength and positivity instead of letting it bring you down? Think about moments when you've felt challenged and what you learned from them.

PRAYER

Dear God, please give me the strength to stand tall in the face of bullying and the courage to treat others with kindness even when it's hard. Help me remember that I am not alone and that Your love surrounds me.

Your worth is not defined by someone else's opinion of you.

OCTOBER 28

CRUSHES AND BOUNDARIES

"There is no fear in love, but perfect love casts out fear."
1 John 4:18

DEVOTIONAL

Sometimes, the best way to handle a crush is to give it time and space; respecting boundaries can lead to something even greater.

What does having a crush feel like for you, and how do you think setting boundaries can help you navigate those feelings in a healthy way?

PRAYER

God, please guide me in understanding my feelings and help me build healthy boundaries that honor both myself and others. Thank you for being my support as I grow. Amen.

Crushes can spark joy, but boundaries keep the heart safe.

DATING WITH RESPECT

"Love is patient and kind; it doesn't boast or make one another feel small. In dating, being respectful means showing genuine consideration for each other." **1 Corinthians 13:4-5**

DEVOTIONAL

Respecting others in dating is about standing up for them, even when it's tough, because everyone deserves to be treated with dignity.

What does it mean to you to respect someone you're interested in dating, and how can you show that respect in your actions and words?

PRAYER

Dear God, help me to remember the value of respect in each relationship I pursue. May I treat others with kindness and integrity, reflecting Your love in every interaction.

Respect is the foundation of every healthy relationship.

OCTOBER 30

WHY PURITY STILL MATTERS

Marriage should be honored by all, and the marriage bed kept pure, for God will judge the adulterer and all the sexually immoral. **Hebrews 13:4**

DEVOTIONAL

Purity isn't just an outdated idea; it's a way to build real relationships based on respect and trust that will stand the test of time.

What does purity mean to you in your life right now, and how do you see it shaping your relationships and your future? Can you think of a moment where choosing purity brought you peace or clarity?

PRAYER

Lord, help me to understand the importance of purity in my life. Teach me to value my choices and to seek a heart that reflects your love and truth. Amen.

Purity is not just about avoiding the wrong choices;
it's about making room for the right ones.

GOD'S VIEW ON LOVE

Love does no harm to a neighbor. Therefore love is the fulfillment of the law.
Romans 13:10

DEVOTIONAL

Love isn't just about feelings; it's about how we treat those around us and the choices we make every day.

What do you think love truly means to you? How do you see love expressed in your life and the lives of those around you?

PRAYER

Dear God, thank you for showing us what true love looks like. Help us to understand and express love in ways that reflect Your heart. May we grow in our capacity to love others and ourselves.

Purity is not just about avoiding the wrong choices; it's about making room for the right ones.

Love is not just a feeling; it's a choice and a commitment that shapes who we are.

WHEN I FEEL REJECTED

What, then, shall we say in response to these things? If God is for us, who can be against us? **Romans 8:31**

DEVOTIONAL

Just because one door closes, it doesn't mean God isn't opening another—trust that you have value beyond the labels others put on you.

What are some moments when you've felt rejected, and how did that influence the way you see yourself and your relationships?

PRAYER

God, thank you for always being with me, even in moments of rejection. Help me to understand my worth through Your eyes and to lean on Your love when I feel alone.

Rejection doesn't define me; it refines me.

GUARDING MY HEART

The heart is deceitful above all things and beyond cure. Who can understand it? **Jeremiah 17:9**

DEVOTIONAL

You have the power to choose who influences you and what you let in; protect your heart like it's your most prized possession.

What influences or distractions in your life do you feel could be affecting the way you guard your heart?

PRAYER

Dear God, help me to recognize what's truly valuable and to keep my heart safe from negativity. Guide me in making choices that honor You and bring peace to my spirit.

Your heart is the wellspring of life; protect it with purpose.

BEING THE RIGHT PERSON FIRST

Dear children, let us not love with words or speech but with actions and in truth. **1 John 3:18**

DEVOTIONAL
The way you treat others defines who you are more than your accomplishments ever will.

What qualities do you think are most important to grow within yourself before you can be the type of friend or leader you aspire to be?

PRAYER
God, help me to become the person I need to be before I focus on who I want to be around. Guide me in my journey to grow in kindness, integrity, and strength. Amen.

> Before seeking the right people around you,
> focus on becoming the right person yourself.

NOVEMBER 4

LUST VS. LOVE

Flee the evil desires of youth and pursue righteousness, faith, love and peace, along with those who call on the Lord out of a pure heart. **2 Timothy 2:22**

DEVOTIONAL
True love requires effort and commitment, while lust is an empty rush that fades away.

What does love look like in your relationships, and how can you tell the difference between it and lust? Think about a time when you felt truly connected to someone versus a moment when your feelings were more physical. How do these experiences shape your views on love?

PRAYER
Dear God, help me to understand the true meaning of love and to seek connections that honor You. Guide me in my relationships, so I can choose the path of love over lust. Amen.

> True love is patient, kind, and seeks to uplift the other person,
> while lust often takes and consumes.

RESPECTING GIRLS AS SISTERS

So in everything, do to others what you would have them do to you, for this sums up the Law and the Prophets. **Matthew 7:12**

DEVOTIONAL

Every girl you meet is someone's sister; treat them with the respect you'd want for your own.

What does it mean to you to treat the girls in your life like sisters? How can respecting them change how you interact with them and the other people around you?

PRAYER

Dear God, thank you for the girls in my life. Help me to see them as my sisters, valuing their thoughts and feelings as I grow in respect and kindness towards them.

To respect a girl is to empower a sister.

NOVEMBER 6

CHOOSING CHARACTER OVER COOLNESS

But test them all; hold on to what is good, reject every kind of evil.
1 Thessalonians 5:21-22

DEVOTIONAL

Character is what you choose when no one is watching; choose it, and you'll rise above the noise.

What does it mean to you to be cool? Are there times when you feel pressured to act a certain way or make choices just to fit in? How can you choose character over coolness in those moments?

PRAYER

Dear God, help me to recognize the value of my character over the fleeting allure of being cool. Strengthen my heart to make choices that reflect my true self and honor You. Guide me in every situation to stand for what is right.

Coolness fades, but character lasts a lifetime.

FAITH WHEN LIFE GETS BORING

Never be lacking in zeal, but keep your spiritual fervor, serving the Lord.
Romans 12:11

DEVOTIONAL

In times of boredom, look for new adventures and opportunities to grow your faith; they often come in unexpected forms.

What do you do when your days feel like they're dragging on and nothing seems exciting? How can you find a sense of purpose in the routine?

PRAYER

God, help me find joy in the small moments and the mundane. Remind me that even in boredom, Your presence is with me and You have a plan for my life.

Even in the mundane, God is working behind the scenes.

DEALING WITH REGRET

For God did not send his Son into the world to condemn the world, but to save the world through him. **John 3:17**

DEVOTIONAL

Don't let past regrets define you; instead, use them as fuel to create a better future.

What is one choice you made in the past that you wish you could change, and how can you learn from that experience instead of letting it define you?

PRAYER

Dear God, thank You for always being there to guide us through our mistakes. Help us to embrace our past, learn from it, and move forward with confidence and hope.

Regret can be a teacher, showing us what truly matters when we take the time to listen.

FOLLOWING CHRIST AT SCHOOL

Be wise in the way you act toward outsiders; make the most of every opportunity. **Colossians 4:5**

DEVOTIONAL

When you choose to follow Christ at school, you have the power to change the atmosphere around you for the better.

What does it mean for you to follow Christ in your school environment, and how do you think your actions can impact those around you? Consider the moments each day where you can shine His light.

PRAYER

Dear God, help me to see every opportunity to represent You at school. Give me strength and courage to be a positive influence on my friends and classmates. Amen.

Your faith in Christ can make waves, changing the atmosphere of your school.

TRUSTING GOD DURING TESTS

"The Lord will fight for you; you need only to be still." **Exodus 14:14**

DEVOTIONAL

Trusting God during tough times can lead you to unexpected victories and peace.

What are some tests you're facing right now, and how can you remind yourself to trust God through them?

PRAYER

Dear God, thank You for being with me in the tough moments. Help me to lean on You and find strength in Your promises as I face my challenges.

Trusting God doesn't mean that we won't face tests;
it means He will be with us every step of the way.

BEING FAITHFUL IN SMALL THINGS

"His master replied, 'Well done, good and faithful servant! You have been faithful with a few things; I will put you in charge of many things. Come and share your master's happiness!'" **Matthew 25:21**

DEVOTIONAL

Success doesn't just happen overnight; it comes from being dedicated and faithful in the small things, even when it's not the most glamorous option.

What small things in your life might God be asking you to be more faithful in? Can you think of a moment this week where being consistent could have made a difference?

PRAYER

Dear God, help me to see the value in the small things and to stay faithful even when no one is watching. Guide me to be diligent in my responsibilities and to trust that you are working through my efforts.

Faithfulness in the little things leads to greater opportunities.

MY IDENTITY IS NOT MY GRADES

So do not throw away your confidence; it will be richly rewarded. You need to persevere so that when you have done the will of God, you will receive what he has promised. **Hebrews 10:35-36**

DEVOTIONAL

Your grades don't define you; how you treat others and pursue your passions does.

What do you think makes you who you are? Is it just about your grades, your popularity, or something deeper? Take a moment to consider the qualities that truly define you.

PRAYER

Dear God, thank You for creating me uniquely and reminding me that my worth goes beyond any letter on a report card. Help me to see myself through Your eyes and to embrace my true identity.

My identity is rooted in who I am, not in what I achieve.

NOVEMBER 13

CHOOSING MY BATTLES

"Do not give dogs what is sacred; do not throw your pearls to pigs. If you do, they may trample them under their feet, and turn and tear you to pieces."
Matthew 7:6

DEVOTIONAL
Choose your battles wisely, focusing on what really builds you up and helps you grow.

What are some battles in your life that truly matter to you? Can you think of situations where you spent energy on things that weren't worth it? How can you better discern which conflicts to engage in?

PRAYER
God, help me to see the battles that truly matter in my life. Give me wisdom to choose wisely and courage to stand firm in what is right. Amen.

"Not every fight is worth fighting; choose the ones that lead to growth."

NOVEMBER 14

SPENDING TIME WITH GOD DAILY

The Lord is near to all who call on him, to all who call on him in truth.
Psalm 145:18

DEVOTIONAL
Developing a habit of spending time with God daily prepares you for life's challenges and reminds you of His presence and support.

What would it look like for you to carve out a little space in your day just to hang out with God? How would feeling His presence change the way you go about your daily activities?

PRAYER
Hey God, thanks for being my friend and always being there for me. Help me set aside time to connect with You daily and grow closer to You. Amen.

Seeing God in the small moments can turn an ordinary day into something extraordinary.

WHEN GOD FEELS DISTANT

I call on you, my God, for you will answer me; turn your ear to me and hear my prayer. **Psalm 17:6**

DEVOTIONAL

When God feels distant, it's not because He's gone; sometimes, we just need to pause and remember that He's always listening, even when we struggle to feel His presence.

What do you think might be causing you to feel distant from God right now? Can you recall any moments when you've felt closer, and what was different about those times?

PRAYER

God, I feel distant from You right now, and I'm searching for Your presence. Help me to trust that You are always with me, even when I can't feel it. Draw me back to You and remind me of Your love.

Even when God feels distant, He is never far from those who seek Him.

FAITH ISN'T ALWAYS A FEELING

For in the gospel the righteousness of God is revealed—a righteousness that is by faith from first to last, just as it is written: "The righteous will live by faith." **Romans 1:17**

DEVOTIONAL

Real faith isn't based on what you feel; it's about what you know and choose to believe, especially when things get tough.

What are some times in your life when you felt like God was distant or when believing felt tough? How did you respond to those moments, and what did they teach you about faith?

PRAYER

Dear God, thank You for being with us even when we can't feel Your presence. Help us to trust in Your promises and remain strong in our faith, no matter what challenges we face.

Faith is a choice, not just a feeling.

LEADING WITHOUT A TITLE

But you are not to be like that. Instead, the greatest among you should be like the youngest, and the one who rules like the one who serves. **Luke 22:26**

DEVOTIONAL

Leadership isn't about a title; it's about the choices you make to uplift and support others.

What does it mean to you to lead in your everyday life, even when no one has called you a leader? How can you step up and take initiative in your school, friend group, or family, even if it feels risky?

PRAYER

Dear God, help me to realize that leadership is not about titles but about service. Give me the courage to influence others positively, even in the small things. Amen.

True leadership is often measured by the impact you make, not the title you hold.

NOVEMBER 18

THE POWER OF ENCOURAGEMENT

But encourage one another daily, as long as it is called "Today," so that none of you may be hardened by sin's deceitfulness. **Hebrews 3:13**

DEVOTIONAL

Never underestimate the impact your words can have; a simple encouragement can lift someone from despair to determination.

What's one time recently when you lifted someone up? How did it feel to encourage them, and how might you offer that same support to someone else today?

PRAYER

Dear God, help me to be a source of encouragement to those around me. Teach me to see the worth in others and give me the courage to speak words that lift them up.

Your words have the power to change someone's day, or even their life.

LEARNING TO WAIT

The Lord is good to those whose hope is in him, to the one who seeks him.
Lamentations 3:25

DEVOTIONAL
Good things come to those who are willing to wait and work hard for them.

What are some areas in your life where you find it hard to wait, and how can you trust that God has a good plan for you during those times?

PRAYER
Dear God, help me to embrace the waiting times in my life, seeing them as opportunities to grow in faith and patience. Remind me that you are always at work, even when I can't see it. Amen.

Patience is the quiet strength that prepares us for the big moments ahead.

WHAT REAL STRENGTH LOOKS LIKE

Be strong and take heart, all you who hope in the Lord. **Psalm 31:24**

DEVOTIONAL
Real strength is found in perseverance and uplifting others,
not just in physical abilities.

What does it mean to be truly strong? Do you think real strength lies in muscles, or could it be about how you treat others and face challenges? Consider moments when you felt strong—what fueled that feeling?

PRAYER
God, help me understand that true strength comes from You. Teach me to be courageous, kind, and resilient in my daily life. Amen.

Real strength is not just about how much you can lift;
it's about how much you can lift others up.

BEING KIND WHEN IT'S HARD

Make sure that nobody pays back wrong for wrong, but always strive to do what is good for each other and for everyone else. **1 Thessalonians 5:15**

DEVOTIONAL
When it's tough to be kind, take a moment to remember that your reaction can turn a hard situation into an opportunity for growth.

What are some difficult situations you've faced recently where being kind felt tough? How did you respond, and what might you do differently next time?

PRAYER
God, help me find the strength to show kindness, especially when it's hard. Teach my heart to choose understanding over frustration, and let my actions reflect Your love. Amen.

Kindness is a choice; it's a superpower you can wield,
even when the world pushes you to do otherwise.

NOVEMBER 22

LETTING GOD CHANGE ME

Do not merely listen to the word, and so deceive yourselves. Do what it says. Anyone who listens to the word but does not do what it says is like someone who looks at his face in a mirror and, after looking at himself, goes away and immediately forgets what he looks like. **James 1:22-24**

DEVOTIONAL
Change starts when we commit to genuinely reflecting on our lives and being intentional in following God's path.

What are some areas in your life where you feel you could let God make a change? How would those changes impact who you are and how you see yourself?

PRAYER
God, I invite you into my heart today. Help me be open to the changes you want to make in my life, and guide me as I trust in your plan. Amen.

Transformation begins the moment you decide to let go and let God.

OBEYING EVEN WHEN I DON'T FEEL LIKE IT

Have confidence in your leaders and submit to their authority, because they keep watch over you as those who must give an account. Do this so that their work will be a joy, not a burden, for that would be of no benefit to you.
Hebrews 13:17

DEVOTIONAL

Sometimes life feels heavy, and doing what's right can seem like an uphill battle, but following through on our commitments can lead to joy and connection in unexpected ways.

What are some situations where you find it hard to obey, and how might your choice to obey, even when you don't feel like it, impact your life and the lives of those around you? Think about a time when you chose to do the right thing against your feelings; what was the outcome?

PRAYER

Dear God, help me remember that obedience is a choice that strengthens my character, even when I don't feel like it. Grant me the courage to follow through with my commitments and to trust Your guidance. Thank You for always being there, cheering me on.

> Obedience is not just about following rules; it's about building a life of trust and integrity.

GOD SEES MY EFFORT

You have searched me, Lord, and you know me. You know when I sit and when I rise; you perceive my thoughts from afar. You discern my going out and my lying down; you are familiar with all my ways. **Psalm 139:1-3**

DEVOTIONAL

God notices every bit of effort you pour into your passions and challenges, even when the results don't show it right away.

What efforts are you putting into your daily life, whether in school, sports, or friendships, that may feel unnoticed? How can you remind yourself that God sees and values your hard work?

PRAYER

Dear God, thank You for always seeing the effort I put in, even when it feels small or unnoticed. Help me to remember that my dedication matters and to find strength in knowing You are with me every step of the way.

> God sees the heart behind your hustle.

FITTING IN VS. STANDING OUT

As water reflects the face, so one's life reflects the heart. **Proverbs 27:19**

DEVOTIONAL

Don't be afraid to show your true colors; being unique can inspire those around you.

What do you think it means to truly fit in, and how might standing out reveal your unique strengths and values?

PRAYER

Dear God, help me embrace who I am and find the courage to stand out when it matters. Remind me that I am unique and valuable, just as you've designed me to be.

Fitting in is temporary; being yourself is timeless.

FINDING REAL JOY

You make known to me the path of life; you will fill me with joy in your presence, with eternal pleasures at your right hand. **Psalm 16:11**

DEVOTIONAL

Real joy isn't found in achievements or accolades, but in the genuine connections and moments we share with those we care about.

What are some things that truly make you feel happy and fulfilled, beyond just the momentary fun? Have you explored deeper sources of joy in your life, such as friendships, family, or your passions?

PRAYER

Dear God, thank you for the joy you bring into our lives. Help me to seek out and embrace the real joy that comes from knowing You and loving others. Amen.

Joy is not just the absence of sadness; it's the presence of something much deeper.

WHEN I'M AFRAID OF THE FUTURE

When I am afraid, I put my trust in you. In God, whose word I praise—in God I trust and am not afraid. What can mere mortals do to me? **Psalm 56:3-4**

DEVOTIONAL

Life is full of uncertainties, but trusting in God helps you navigate through your fears and embrace the future.

What fears do you have about the future, and how do these fears shape the choices you're making today?

PRAYER

God, thank You for being with me in uncertain times. Help me to trust that You have a plan for my life, even when I can't see what lies ahead. Give me courage to face my fears and keep moving forward.

Fear doesn't need to define your future—your faith does.

STAYING CALM UNDER PRESSURE

Fools show their annoyance at once, but the prudent overlook an insult.
Proverbs 12:16

DEVOTIONAL

The next time you feel overwhelmed, remember it's okay to take a step back and breathe before reacting.

What pressures are you facing right now in your life, and how can you respond to them without letting them overwhelm you?

PRAYER

God, help me to find peace in the middle of chaos. Teach me to trust in You when everything around me feels intense and challenging. Give me the strength to stay calm and focused.

Calmness is not the absence of pressure, but the presence of peace.

HELPING WITHOUT EXPECTING CREDIT

Serve wholeheartedly, as if you were serving the Lord, not people.
Ephesians 6:7

DEVOTIONAL

Sometimes the greatest acts of kindness are those we give without looking for anything in return.

What's a time you helped someone without thinking about what you might get in return? How did that feel, and what did you learn from it?

PRAYER

God, help me to serve others with a pure heart, seeking to lift them up without looking for praise in return. Teach me to find joy in giving and to be a light to those around me. Amen.

True strength lies in lifting others up, not seeking to be lifted yourself.

NOVEMBER 30

LETTING GO OF ENVY

For where you have envy and selfish ambition, there you find disorder and every evil practice. **James 3:16**

DEVOTIONAL

Don't let envy steal your joy or hinder your progress; focus on your own journey and let others inspire you instead.

What is one area in your life where you find yourself wishing you had what someone else has? How might you shift your focus toward gratitude instead?

PRAYER

Dear God, help me to release any feelings of jealousy that weigh me down. Fill my heart with gratitude for the blessings in my life and help me celebrate the successes of others.

The grass isn't always greener; sometimes it's just different.

DECEMBER 1

DEALING WITH INJUSTICE

But as for me, my feet had almost slipped; I had nearly lost my foothold. For I envied the arrogant when I saw the prosperity of the wicked. **Psalm 73:2-3**

DEVOTIONAL

Remember, handling injustice is often more about your personal response than the wrong that was done.

What injustices have you faced recently, and how have they affected your thoughts and feelings? Take a moment to consider how you responded to them and what God's perspective might be in those situations.

PRAYER

Dear God, help me to see beyond the injustices I face and to trust in your goodness and fairness. Give me the strength to act justly and support those who are hurting. Amen.

Even in the darkest moments, we can shine a light of justice and hope.

DECEMBER 2

GOD CARES ABOUT MY STRUGGLES

Are not two sparrows sold for a penny? Yet not one of them will fall to the ground outside your Father's care. And even the very hairs of your head are all numbered. So don't be afraid; you are worth more than many sparrows. **Matthew 10:29-31**

DEVOTIONAL

No struggle is too small or insignificant; God notices everything we go through and cares about it all.

What struggles are you facing right now that make you feel overwhelmed or alone? How can you remind yourself that God is walking alongside you in these moments?

PRAYER

Dear God, thank you for always being there for me, even when I feel lost or uncertain. Help me to remember that I'm never alone in my struggles, and give me strength to face whatever challenges come my way.

Even in the toughest battles, you're never fighting alone.

DECEMBER 3

GIVING GOD MY DREAMS

Take delight in the Lord, and he will give you the desires of your heart.
Psalm 37:4

DEVOTIONAL

When you give your dreams to God, He can turn your aspirations into something greater than you ever imagined.

What dreams do you hold in your heart, and how might they look if you handed them over to God?

PRAYER

Dear God, I thank You for the dreams and passions You've planted in my heart. Help me to trust You with my future and guide my steps as I seek to follow Your plan.

Giving God your dreams allows Him to turn them into a reality that far exceeds your imagination.

DECEMBER 4

WHAT TO DO WHEN I'M CONFUSED

"Ask and it will be given to you; seek and you will find; knock and the door will be opened to you." **Matthew 7:7**

DEVOTIONAL

When you're confused, seek guidance and trust that clarity will come with time and effort.

What situations in your life make you feel the most confused, and how do you usually handle those feelings? Think about a recent moment when you didn't know what to do. What would you want to hear from God in that moment?

PRAYER

Dear God, when I feel lost and unsure, help me to lean on You for guidance. Remind me that I am never alone in my confusion, and that You are always ready to listen and lead me. Amen.

Confusion is not the absence of clarity; it's often the beginning of discovery.

DECEMBER 5

LOVING PEOPLE I DISAGREE WITH

Whoever claims to love God yet hates a brother or sister is a liar. For whoever does not love their brother and sister, whom they have seen, cannot love God, whom they have not seen. **1 John 4:20**

DEVOTIONAL
Sometimes, it's more important to love and respect the people around us than to win an argument.

What does it mean to truly love someone you don't see eye to eye with? Can you think of someone in your life that you find it hard to agree with? How can you show them love and respect despite your differences?

PRAYER
God, help me to see others through Your eyes. Give me strength to love those I disagree with, finding common ground in understanding and kindness. Amen.

Love is not about agreement; it's about connection.

DECEMBER 6

THE POWER OF FORGIVENESS

"I, even I, am he who blots out your transgressions, for my own sake, and remembers your sins no more." **Isaiah 43:25**

DEVOTIONAL
Forgiveness isn't just about letting someone else off the hook; it's about freeing yourself to live life with joy and lightness.

What does forgiveness mean to you, and how can it change your life and your relationships with others? Consider a time when you struggled to forgive someone. What would it look like to let go of that burden?

PRAYER
Dear God, thank you for the gift of forgiveness. Help me to find the strength to forgive others and to embrace Your grace in my own life. Guide me as I learn to let go and grow.

Forgiveness is the key that unlocks the door of resentment and the handcuffs of hatred.

BEING GRATEFUL EVERY DAY

Give thanks to the Lord, for he is good; his love endures forever.
1 Chronicles 16:34

DEVOTIONAL
When you make gratitude a habit, it changes how
you see the world around you.

*What are three things you can be grateful for today, and how can
focusing on those things change your perspective on life right now?*

PRAYER
Dear God, thank you for the many blessings you give us each day,
both big and small. Help me to see the good in my life and to
cultivate a grateful heart that shines through in my actions.

Gratitude transforms what we have into enough.

WHAT MAKES A REAL MAN

The righteous lead blameless lives; blessed are their children after them.
Proverbs 20:7

DEVOTIONAL
Being a real man isn't about looking tough or fitting in; it's about standing up
for what's right and living with integrity.

*What does being a real man mean to you? Think about the qualities you
admire in others and how you can embody those traits in your own life.
What steps can you take today to develop your character and integrity?*

PRAYER
Dear God, help me understand what it means to be a real man. Guide my
heart and my actions so I can grow into the person you want me to be.
Amen.

Being a real man is not about being tough; it's about being true.

REJECTING LABELS

There is neither Jew nor Gentile, neither slave nor free, nor is there male and female, for you are all one in Christ Jesus. **Galatians 3:28**

DEVOTIONAL

You are not defined by the labels others give you; embrace your unique identity and passions instead.

What labels have people placed on you, and how do they make you feel about yourself? Are these identities authentic, or do they limit who you really are? Take a moment to think about what you want to be known for.

PRAYER

Dear God, help me to see beyond the labels others put on me. Teach me to embrace my true self and live out the identity You have given me. Amen.

> You are not defined by what others say about you,
> but by who you choose to become.

DECEMBER 10

GOD CAN USE MY PAIN

You intended to harm me, but God intended it for good to accomplish what is now being done, the saving of many lives. **Genesis 50:20**

DEVOTIONAL

Your struggles are not in vain; they can lead to something greater that can help others if you keep pushing forward and trust God with your journey.

What pain or struggle are you facing right now that you can trust God to use for something greater in your life? How can you allow this experience to shape you instead of define you?

PRAYER

God, I bring my pain and struggles to you today. Help me to see how you can use these moments to grow and strengthen me. Open my eyes to your purpose in my life.

> Your pain is not just a burden; it's a bridge to your growth and others' healing.

DECEMBER 11

WHEN I FEEL SPIRITUALLY DRY

Then Jesus told his disciples a parable to show them that they should always pray and not give up. **Luke 18:1**

DEVOTIONAL
When you're feeling spiritually dry, remember that showing up in prayer and community can renew your connection to God.

What do you think causes you to feel spiritually dry, and how can you seek renewal in those moments?

PRAYER
God, I may feel distant from You right now, but I ask You to draw me close. Help me to find refreshment in Your presence and the strength to keep seeking You.

Even the strongest trees need rain to thrive; it's okay to ask for help when you're feeling parched.

DECEMBER 12

CARING FOR THE LEAST POPULAR

But when you give a banquet, invite the poor, the crippled, the lame, the blind, and you will be blessed. Although they cannot repay you, you will be repaid at the resurrection of the righteous." **Luke 14:13-14**

DEVOTIONAL
Sometimes, the least popular kids are the ones who need your friendship the most, so don't be afraid to step up and include them.

What does it mean to you to reach out to someone who seems overlooked or not included? How might you show kindness to that person this week?

PRAYER
Dear God, thank you for your unconditional love. Help me to see the value in everyone and give me the courage to reach out to those who need a friend.

Your kindness can be the light in someone else's darkness.

DECEMBER 13

AVOIDING GOSSIP

The words of a gossip are like choice morsels; they go down
to the inmost parts. **Proverbs 18:8**

DEVOTIONAL

Respect and kindness matter more than fitting in, so choose to uplift others
instead of tearing them down.

*What does it feel like when someone talks about you behind your back, and
how can you choose to lift others up instead of tearing them down?*

PRAYER

Dear God, help me to be mindful of my words. Let my conversations be filled
with kindness and truth, and give me the strength to avoid the temptation of
gossip.

Words have the power to build bridges or walls;
choose wisely which ones you lay down.

DECEMBER 14

WHY CHURCH MATTERS

Let the message of Christ dwell among you richly as you teach and
admonish one another with all wisdom through psalms, hymns, and songs
from the Spirit, singing to God with gratitude in your hearts. **Colossians 3:16**

DEVOTIONAL

Sometimes, the best church experience happens outside of a building,
highlighting the importance of community in building your faith.

*What do you think makes a community so important in your life, and how do
you feel about being part of a church community?*

PRAYER

God, thank You for the gift of community. Help me see the value in being part
of the church and encourage me to grow in faith with others around me.

Being part of a church isn't just about attending; it's
about belonging to something bigger than yourself.

WHY BAPTISM MATTERS

Jesus answered, "Very truly I tell you, no one can enter the kingdom of God unless they are born of water and the Spirit." **John 3:5**

DEVOTIONAL

Baptism isn't just a ritual; it's the ultimate sign of your commitment to a life with purpose and connection to something greater.

What does baptism mean to you personally, and how do you think it reflects your relationship with God?

PRAYER

Dear God, thank you for the gift of baptism and the chance to declare our faith. Help me to understand its meaning in my life and to embrace the journey ahead with courage and joy.

Baptism is not just a ritual; it's a declaration of a new identity in Christ.

DECEMBER 16

LIVING THE GOSPEL, NOT JUST PREACHING IT

Whatever happens, conduct yourselves in a manner worthy of the gospel of Christ. Then, whether I come and see you or only hear about you in my absence, I will know that you stand firm in the one Spirit, striving together as one for the faith of the gospel. **Philippians 1:27**

DEVOTIONAL

What you say about your faith needs to show up in how you live your life every day. Don't just talk the talk – walk the walk, and remember that people are always watching. Live out your faith in everything you do, so that your actions reflect the Gospel you believe in.

What does it mean for you to actually live out what you believe every day, beyond just talking about it? Can you think of a moment when your actions spoke louder than your words?

PRAYER

God, help me to live out Your love and truth in my daily life. Let my actions reflect my faith so that others can see You in me. Thank You for guiding me as I strive to be a true example of Your Gospel.

Your life is the sermon that others will hear long before they read the scriptures.

DECEMBER 17

AVOIDING DOUBLE LIFE

Jesus Christ is the same yesterday and today and forever. **Hebrews 13:8**

DEVOTIONAL

Being authentic makes life easier and more fulfilling than pretending to be someone you're not. This means you don't have to change who you are depending on where you are or who you're with. Whether you're at school, with friends, or at home, staying true to yourself and your faith is crucial.

What areas of your life feel divided? Are there parts of yourself you hide from others, or things you do when no one's watching that don't align with who you want to be? Take a moment to think about how you can bring those pieces together.

PRAYER

Lord, help me to know and embrace my true self. Guide me to live authentically and boldly, letting go of the masks I wear. Amen.

Living authentically means embracing who you are in both the light and the shadows.

DECEMBER 18

BEING A LIGHT ONLINE

We are therefore Christ's ambassadors, as though God were making his appeal through us. We implore you on Christ's behalf: Be reconciled to God. **2 Corinthians 5:20**

DEVOTIONAL

Remember, your words have the power to either tear down or build up—choose to be the light that brightens someone's day. When you're scrolling or posting online, you're representing something way bigger than yourself.

What does it mean for you to be a light in the online world? How can your actions and words uplift those around you, even in a digital space where it's easy to hide or blend in?

PRAYER

Dear God, help me to shine Your light through my online interactions. Give me the strength to choose kindness and encouragement, and let my presence be a source of hope to others. Amen.

Shining your light online can change someone's day, just as a single spark can ignite a fire.

NOT JUST A SUNDAY CHRISTIAN

"Therefore everyone who hears these words of mine and puts them into practice is like a wise man who built his house on the rock. The rain came down, the streams rose, and the winds blew and beat against that house; yet it did not fall, because it had its foundation on the rock. **Matthew 7:24-25**

DEVOTIONAL

If you want your faith to be solid, make sure it's not just a Sunday routine but a part of everything you do.

What does it mean to you to live your faith every day, not just on Sunday? How can you make your actions reflect your beliefs in school, with friends, and at home?

PRAYER

God, help me to live out my faith beyond Sunday. Teach me to be a light in every situation, showing love and kindness to those around me. Thank you for being with me every step of the way.

Faith is not just a Sunday feeling; it's a Tuesday action and a Friday choice.

DECEMBER 20

BEING CONSISTENT WITH MY WORDS

Those who guard their mouths and their tongues keep themselves from calamity. **Proverbs 21:23**

DEVOTIONAL

Words matter, and staying true to what you say brings strength to your character.

What do you think happens when your words don't match your actions? How would that affect your relationships with your friends, family, and even yourself?

PRAYER

Dear God, help me to be mindful of my words today. Teach me to speak with honesty and kindness, so my words reflect who I truly want to be. Amen.

Words are powerful; they can build others up or tear them down.

DECEMBER 21

FINDING GOD IN NATURE

The heavens declare the glory of God; the skies proclaim the work of his hands. Day after day they pour forth speech; night after night they reveal knowledge. They have no speech, they use no words; no sound is heard from them. Yet their voice goes out into all the earth, their words to the ends of the world. In the heavens God has pitched a tent for the sun. **Psalm 19:1-4**

DEVOTIONAL

God speaks through the beauty of the world around you; take a moment to step outside and listen.

What elements of nature do you find most inspiring or comforting? How can you take time this week to connect with God through the beauty around you?

PRAYER

God, thank you for the beauty of your creation. Help me to see you in the world around me, and guide me to moments of peace and inspiration through nature.

Nature whispers the presence of God to those who take the time to listen.

DECEMBER 22

CHOOSING PEACE OVER DRAMA

Turn from evil and do good; seek peace and pursue it. **Psalm 34:14**

DEVOTIONAL

In a world full of noise and chaos, choosing to be a peacemaker can make all the difference for you and those around you.

What situations in your life currently feel like they're overflowing with drama? How can you choose peace instead?

PRAYER

Dear God, help me to find your peace in moments of chaos. Teach me to respond with calmness instead of getting swept away in drama. May I reflect your love and understanding in all my interactions.

Peace isn't the absence of conflict, but the presence of a calm heart amid it all.

DECEMBER 23

WHEN GOD SAYS WAIT

For the revelation awaits an appointed time; it speaks of the end and will not prove false. Though it linger, wait for it; it will certainly come and will not delay.
Habakkuk 2:3

DEVOTIONAL
The waiting period can be a time of growth, as God often teaches us lessons that will help us make the most of what's coming next.

What are some areas in your life right now where you feel like you're being asked to wait, and how does that make you feel?

PRAYER
God, help me to trust in Your timing and find peace during this waiting season. May I grow in patience and understanding, knowing that You have a plan for my life. Amen.

Waiting isn't wasting time; it's preparing you for something greater.

DECEMBER 24

FOCUSING ON GOD'S VOICE

Dear friends, do not believe every spirit, but test the spirits to see whether they are from God, because many false prophets have gone out into the world. **1 John 4:1**

DEVOTIONAL
The real victory lies in listening to God's voice and sticking up for what you believe, even when it's tough.

What distractions are keeping you from tuning in to God's voice? How can you carve out a moment today to seek Him in the midst of your busy life?

PRAYER
God, help me to quiet my heart and mind so I can hear Your voice. Teach me to recognize Your presence in my day-to-day life and guide me in the direction You want me to go. Amen.

Listening to God is the key to unlocking the doors of your purpose.

DECEMBER 25

TRUSTING GOD WITH MY TALENTS

Then the Lord said to him, "What is that in your hand?" "A staff," he replied. The Lord said, "Throw it on the ground." Moses threw it on the ground and it became a snake, and he ran from it. **Exodus 4:2-3**

DEVOTIONAL
Your talents aren't about being the best; they're about stepping up and using what God has given you, no matter how small it seems.

What talents do you have that you might be holding back? How can you take a step today to trust God with those gifts and use them for something greater?

PRAYER
Dear God, thank You for the talents You've given me. Help me to embrace them and use them wisely, always seeking to glorify You in all that I do.

Your talents are gifts from God; what you do with them can change the world.

DECEMBER 26

BEING KNOWN BY MY LOVE

Jesus replied: "'Love the Lord your God with all your heart and with all your soul and with all your mind.' This is the first and greatest commandment. And the second is like it: 'Love your neighbor as yourself.'" **Matthew 22:37-39**

DEVOTIONAL
You don't have to be front and center to be truly known; it's about being genuine and loving, both yourself and others.

What does it feel like to truly know someone, and how can you show that same love to those around you? How does being known for who you are shape the way you love others?

PRAYER
Dear God, thank you for the love you have shown me. Help me to reflect that love in my relationships and to be known for kindness and authenticity. Amen.

Being known means being loved for who you really are, not just for what others see.

DECEMBER 27

STANDING FIRM IN TEMPTATION

Be alert and of sober mind. Your enemy the devil prowls around like a roaring lion looking for someone to devour. Resist him, standing firm in the faith, because you know that the family of believers throughout the world is undergoing the same kind of sufferings. **1 Peter 5:8-9**

DEVOTIONAL

Remember, standing firm might mean going against the flow, but it's your integrity and courage that will define you in the long run.

What temptations are you facing today, and how can you find strength to resist them?

PRAYER

Dear God, please help me to stand firm when I feel tempted. Give me the courage to choose what is right and the wisdom to seek Your strength in every challenge I face.

True strength is not just about resisting temptation but knowing who you are in Christ.

DECEMBER 28

LETTING GOD SHAPE MY IDENTITY

I have been crucified with Christ and I no longer live, but Christ lives in me. The life I now live in the body, I live by faith in the Son of God, who loved me and gave himself for me. **Galatians 2:20**

DEVOTIONAL

Letting God shape your identity frees you to be the authentic version of yourself, unburdened by the need for others' approval.

What do you believe defines who you are right now, and how might God's perspective change that for you?

PRAYER

God, help me see myself through Your eyes. Teach me to embrace who I am as Your creation and to let Your love shape my understanding of my identity.

Your true identity is found not in what you do, but in who you are in Christ.

HOW TO SAY SORRY

"If you forgive anyone's sins, their sins are forgiven; if you do not forgive them, they are not forgiven." **John 20:23**

DEVOTIONAL

Learning to say sorry isn't a weakness; it's a powerful step toward building stronger relationships.

What's one situation where you know you need to apologize but haven't found the right moment yet? How could saying sorry change your relationship?

PRAYER

Dear God, help me find the courage to say sorry when I hurt others. Let my words bring healing and restore the bonds of friendship. Thank you for your endless grace and forgiveness.

Apology is not a sign of weakness; it's a step towards strength and maturity.

OVERCOMING LAZINESS

A sluggard's appetite is never filled, but the desires of the diligent are fully satisfied. **Proverbs 13:4**

DEVOTIONAL

Success comes to those who put in the effort, so choose to act today instead of waiting for tomorrow.

What are some things you've been putting off lately because it feels easier to just chill out instead of getting things done?

PRAYER

God, help me break free from laziness and take steps toward my goals. Give me the motivation to act, and remind me that every small effort counts. Thank you for always being by my side.

Taking the first step is always the hardest, but it's also the most important.

TAKING CARE OF MY BODY

Proverbs 3:7-8

DEVOTIONAL
You can't go hard all the time; learning to balance pushing yourself with taking care of your body is the real game changer.

What does it mean to you to take care of your body, both physically and mentally? When you think about your goals, how do your habits support or challenge those dreams?

PRAYER
Dear God, thank You for the gift of my body and the strength I find in taking care of it. Help me to make choices that honor You and reflect the potential You've placed within me. Guide me in my journey toward health and wellness.

My body is a temple, a place where strength, resilience, and purpose collide.

DID THIS DEVOTIONAL MAKE A DIFFERENCE?

Hey Brother,

If these daily devotionals have helped you grow in confidence, courage, or faith, I'd be grateful if you shared your experience with others.

Your review on Amazon can help more teen boys discover this book and start their own journey toward a stronger faith and purpose.

To leave your review, just scan the QR code below with your phone's camera, or type the link into your computer or phone's browser.

https://go.binnovatedigital.com/TeenBoysDevotional